SHOOT! ANNUAL 1988

ANSWERS PAGE 127

GARY LINEKER

Gary sprung to world wide fame with his performances for England in the 1986 World Cup Finals. After a season at Everton he had a dream move to Spanish giants Barcelona in '86.

1. Lineker cracked a hat-trick for England against which Group F rivals in the '86 World Cup Finals?

2. How many goals did Gary score in the tournament and did he finish top scorer in the Finals?

3. Gary made his debut for England in 1984 against Scotland and scored his first goal for his country against Eire in 1985. True or false?

4. Lineker started his League career at which club?

5. Can you name the match and the opposition when Gary scored his last goal for Everton in May '86?

IAN RUSH

The best finisher in the game today? Many think so. Certainly Italian giants Juventus who paid a staggering £3.2 million to capture the former Liverpool star do.

1. Rush's millionaire move to Juventus is a long way from where he started his career. Name his first League club?

2. Ian made his international debut for Wales in 1980 against Norway, Iceland or Scotland?

3. Did Rush ever play a competitive match for Liverpool against Juventus before joining the Italian club?

4. Rush's first goal for Wales was against the Republic of Ireland in 1982. True or False?

5. Ian has formed a lethal partnership for Wales with which aggressive striker?

£3·50

Gary Lineker recalls the night he

THE ASS

People have kindly dubbed me one of the world's best strikers. I still find it difficult to believe that I can be mentioned in the same breath as the Laudrups, Rushes, Rummenigges, and Butraguenos.

Hey, it is only eight years since I stepped nervously into the Leicester first team and only three and a half years since I faced the thunderous roar of a Hampden Park crowd in winning my first England cap as substitute.

But my short and fascinating career, full of thrills from all corners of the world, has given me enough time to realise that there are some fairly difficult defenders to overcome if I am to maintain my reputation as a world class striker.

People say to me: "Which defender do you fear most?"

I am not sure I am frightened of anyone, but I know what they mean. So, taking their lead, I have given considerable thought to naming the hit squad I am happy to avoid.

The player I have a great deal of respect for is Spanish international defender Juan Carlos Arteche.

The last time I played against the iron-hard Atletico Madrid defender they

call The Assassin in an international match, I destroyed him!

That's what worries me. There is no way Mr Arteche, one of the toughest defenders in world football, will allow me to have so much freedom again.

Mr Arteche has never forgotten a bitterly cold night in Madrid in February 1987 when I pumped four goals past him for England against Spain.

It was billed as a 'friendly' but Mr Arteche was not smiling when the final whistle blew in the mighty Bernabeu Stadium.

Spain 2, England 4 said the electronic scoreboard to the delight of a healthy contingent of England fans.

The world is full of hard tackling and difficult defenders like The Assassin. Jose Luis Brown, the Argentinian with the English sounding name, has all the right credentials to become as famous as his international team-mate Passarella.

Although I have played a lot of international football, I still remember titanic battles with men I respect in the English First Division.

Nearly every team in the First Division has a strong central defender who makes life difficult for all but the sharpest strikers.

I always found Terry Butcher, my England team-mate an 'Everest', when he ran the Ipswich defence. He is now shoring-up the mighty Rangers in the Ibrox Stadium.

I always thought myself lucky to be playing *with* Kevin Ratcliffe rather than *against* him when we played together at Everton.

Trying to outwit or outpace Ratty in a five-a-side game was like trying to crack the wall of the Kremlin with a wooden hammer. He doesn't look as menacing as Arteche but there is bite in every tackle.

His greatest asset in leading the Welsh defence is his pace. You can beat him once but before you can get away, he is snapping at your heels again.

The new Rolls-Royce of the First Division is Tony Adams from reports I receive from England.

Family and friends pop over to Barcelona to bring Michelle and me all the news.

Tony made his England debut on the

day I scored all four in Madrid. I wondered then whether he would make a future England captain. He has tremendous leadership qualities for one so young, pointing, shouting and generally getting people organised.

The Arsenal defender, born in London just after England won the World Cup, has come right through the England ranks, from Schoolboy, Youth and

Under-21 levels to win full honours.

He tells me he still likes a kick-around with the lads he lives near in Rainham, Essex. He isn't the first England star to play park football with soccer crazy kids from his neighbourhood but it shows Tony's love of the game.

Paul McGrath, Manchester United's Republic of Ireland defender, has everything. Pace, power, grace, competitiveness . . . it's all wrapped together in a 6ft, 13 stone frame that gets better and better.

One of the mysteries of international

Gary's former team-mate Kevin Ratcliffe.

4

estroyed
ASSIN!

The third of Gary's four goals against Spain in Madrid.

selection is why Alan Hansen, Liverpool's centre-back, has won so few caps for Scotland.

The answer, of course, is that Willie Miller and Alex McLeish placed a stranglehold on the number 5 and 6 shirt up to the 1986 World Cup Finals!

Sadly, Alan, born in June 1955, is hardly likely to finish with 30 Scotland caps, a major disappointment for a lad who looked to have everything when I struggled to puncture the Liverpool defence during my Leicester City and Everton days.

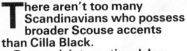

There aren't too many Scandinavians who possess broader Scouse accents than Cilla Black.

Denmark international Jan Molby, though, wouldn't appear unrealistic if he landed a speaking part in a Carla Lane sit-com.

Molby's Mersey twang isn't in itself a vital ingredient to his footballing make-up, but in its own way gives an illustration of how well he has adapted at Liverpool.

Certainly Molby's name can be included on a list of Football League imports who have proved themselves successful in the First Division.

He is Anfield's Great Dane, yet there was a time when a group of cynics labelled him the Late Dane after his arrival at Anfield in a £220,000 transfer from Ajax in August 1984.

Signed by former Liverpool boss Joe Fagan to plug the gap left by the influential Graeme Souness — who joined Sampdoria in Italy before making a massive impact in Scottish football as manager of Rangers — Molby is the first to admit he wasn't an instant success.

His previous experiences of the game in Holland and with his home-town club of Kolding in Denmark were a far cry from

IELD'S
AT DANE

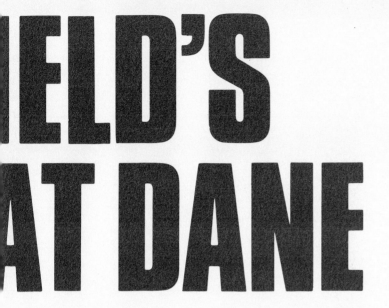

the frantic pressures of the English First Division.

At the end of that 1984–85 season the Anfield trophy cupboard was bare for the first time since 1975.

Molby recalls: ''I knew comparisons between Graeme Souness and myself would be inevitable.

''But I don't think they were fair all the same because I'm not the same sort of player as Souness and I never will be.''

Ian Rush, Molby's former team-mate at Anfield before joining Juventus, points out: ''I think people tended to forget that Jan was only 21 when he first joined Liverpool.

''To heap pressure on him about Graeme Souness at that age was terribly unfair.

''But Jan showed his courage by overcoming any initial problems and winning over the fans.''

Several adjustments had to be made to Molby's game before he started to fulfil his obvious potential.

And Kenny Dalglish had a helping hand when he made Steve McMahon his first signing as manager, to take over the ball-winning duties and release Molby into a more creative role.

Rush adds: ''I remember talking to Jan about it, and he told me how different the English game was to anything he had previously encountered.

''He said the First Division was about 100 times faster than anything he'd been used to. He also complained that within a split second of receiving the ball he'd find himself having to contend with a couple of opponents challenging him for the ball.''

As Molby's Scouse accent developed, so it seemed did his ability to command a midfield in the Football League.

Vital

Rush continues: ''After being just a squad player Jan became a vital member of the first-team. It seemed that Liverpool were only playing well when Jan Molby was on form.

''And that must be the final proof of how well he has adapted to our game.''

So what are Molby's strengths? Rush grabbed many a goal after connecting to a Molby pass.

He says: ''Jan could play a pass to your feet accurately.

''Jan can also weight a pass so beautifully so that the ball seems to sit up nicely for you just as you're about to strike it.

''And Jan possesses an extremely powerful shot with both feet, and is particularly dangerous around the box.

''But perhaps the most surprising thing about Jan is his skill on the ball. I can't think of many big lads with the finesse on the ball that he has.''

Certainly Molby's talent didn't go unnoticed at Rush's new club Juventus, who were seriously considering a bid for him before Kenny Dalglish stepped in with a new five year contract.

The signing of Steve McMahon from Aston Villa released Molby into a more creative role.

Charlie Nicholas reveals...

It's It

Maradona the "king" of Napoli.

someone like George Best or Pele could have made if they had been playing in Italy today.

But more important than money is happiness, and that's why I'm not going to rush into anything.

I had a lot of problems when I first moved down from Celtic. It took me a long time to settle in London and I found it hard to distinguish between genuine friends and hangers-on.

A move to Italy would be an even bigger upheaval, so it's essential I fix myself up with the right club.

I want to be part of a team whose style will suit my own game, because I've seen how lads like Luther Blissett and Mark Hateley have been slaughtered by the hyper-critical Italian press when the goals dried up.

But as I say, that's all in the future. At the moment I just want to prove myself in the Football League and win a regular place in the Scotland team.

People who believe that the Football League is still the best in the world are behind the times. For the First Division is now second best to Italy's 'Serie A'.

And that's why I intend to try my luck in the Mediterranean sunshine at some stage of my career.

You only have to look at the star names who have been lured to Italy to realise that they now provide the ultimate soccer challenge.

Maradona, Platini, Rummenigge, Brady, Laudrup and Zico have all left their countrymen behind to lap it up in the land of the lire.

But the man who has really convinced me that my future also lies in Italy is Ian Rush.

Rushie is the finest goalscorer in the world . . . bar none. He is going to be a sensation at Juventus and if it's good enough for him then it's certainly good enough for me.

But don't get me wrong. I'm not packing my bags this minute. I reckon it will be a couple of years yet before I'm ready to catch that plane.

First of all I know I must do the business in England. The Italians don't want any old rubbish.

But I know that if I don't get out there before I retire I'll regret it for the rest of my life. I'll always wonder whether or not I could have made it with the best in the world.

I played there a couple of times during European ties for Celtic and the atmosphere was just incredible. Soccer is like a religion to the Italian fans.

They treat the players like gods and pay them accordingly. And I'd be a liar if I didn't admit that the extraordinary wages they offer would be part of the attraction for me.

I would be stupid to ignore the money on offer. A player can set himself up financially for the rest of his life.

I sometimes wonder how much

Laudrup of Juventus clashes with A.C. Milan's Paolo Maldini.

aly for me!

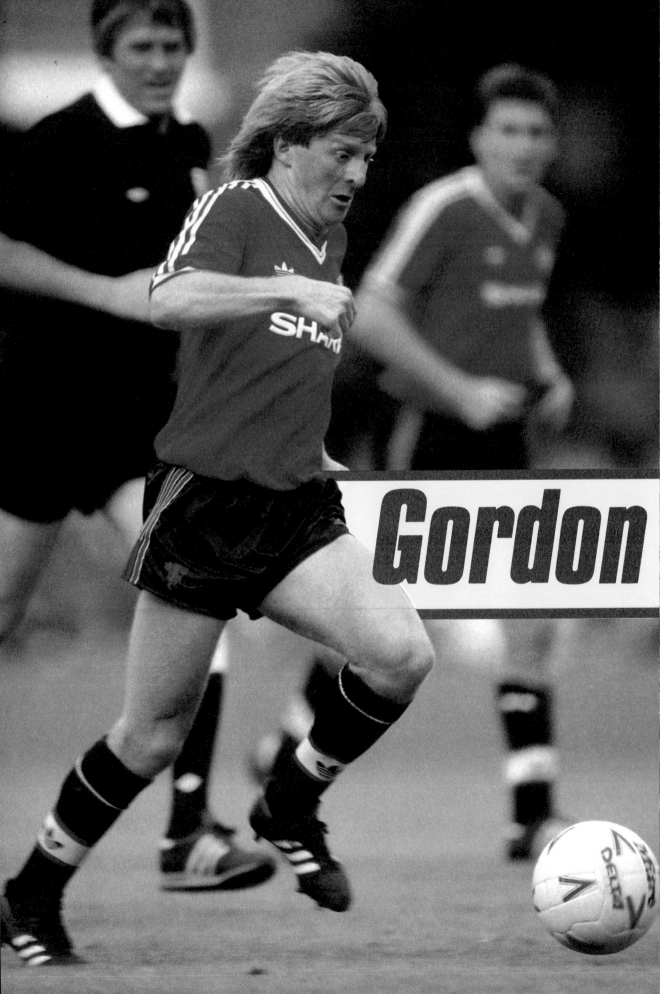

Gordon

There was a time early on in Gordon Strachan's career when, by his own admission, he was probably a little too tough for his own good.

The flame haired Scotland international raises a smile as he recalls one match for his first club Dundee against local rivals Dundee United.

He remembers: ''United's team included twins Jimmy and Sandy White, and one of them caught me with a particularly bad foul that sent me crashing to the ground.

''I leapt up immediately to find them both standing in front of me. There was no way of knowing which one was the culprit — they were absolutely identical.

''There was only one thing for it, I decided, so I went for both of them. I was sent off.''

Strachan, more than ten years older and wiser, now intends to channel his aggression in the accepted way.

He was once described by former Manchester United manager Ron Atkinson as ''the magician'' — and few among the many thousands who pack Old Trafford every other Saturday would disagree.

But Strachan believes the arrival

United's Eire star Paul McGrath is one of Europe's most complete defenders.

gets tough

at Old Trafford last season of new boss Alex Ferguson will add another dimension to his game to help United to a long overdue League Championship triumph.

Ferguson, who was Strachan's boss at Aberdeen, is renowned as a strict disciplinarian. And few welcome a more tougher image for United than Strachan.

He says: ''I have believed for a while now that we must toughen-up our attitude if we want to really compete in Championship races.''

Too often in recent seasons United's buccaneering style has cost them dear. How many times, for example, can you recall watching them surrender a two goal lead in televised matches?

Strachan admits: ''It hasn't always been in the nature of teams at Manchester United to kill off a match.

''Even when we've been leading there has been something in us

that urges us forward blindly in search of more goals.

''But sides like Liverpool have the ability to hold on to their lead more often than not. And they can point to plenty of silverware in their trophy cabinet as a reward for that style of play.

''I don't think our supporters would stand for it if we went totally the other way and played for 1–0 wins every week.

''But there is little doubt in my mind that we should attack with a little more care. We should also pay more attention to making it as difficult as possible for our opponents to break through.''

United, of course, aren't exactly short on tenacious competitors. Norman Whiteside and Remi Moses have always been ready to add steel to Strachan's skill.

And, in Republic of Ireland star Paul McGrath, Ferguson has inherited one of Europe's most

complete central defenders.

United skipper Bryan Robson believes Ferguson is bringing out the best in Strachan.

He says: ''Gordon worked well with Alex Ferguson when the boss brought him through at Pittodrie, and I can see the same chemistry working between them again.

''Gordon was one of the best players in the game when Ron Atkinson persuaded Alex to part with him in the first place.

''But I sense that, after being reunited with his old boss, Gordon has developed into one of United's best players.

''Gordon is always battling and he refuses to be beaten until the final whistle.''

Champion

Strachan, born in Edinburgh in 1957, first teamed up with Ferguson at Aberdeen in 1977. The pair celebrated two League Championships, three successive Scottish Cup triumphs and a European Cup Winners' Cup success before Strachan signed for United in a £600,000 transfer in 1984.

And it is clear that Gordon Strachan is not prepared to accept second best for much longer. That is bad news for the giants of Merseyside and North London . . .

High AND

Coventry goalkeeper Steve Ogrizovic joined an elite band and achieved a personal ambition when he scored a goal against Sheffield Wednesday.

His huge clearance kick, assisted by a gale force wind, soared more than 100 yards and went into the net off a post.

Observers reckoned the punt travelled 107 yards because the Hillsborough pitch is 115 yards long.

Poor Wednesday goalkeeper Martin Hodge was devastated when he attacked the ball only to see it bounce over his head from the edge of the penalty-area.

''A pure fluke,'' said Oggy. ''It does not detract from Martin's skill as a goalkeeper. It could happen to any of us.''

Steve Ogrizovic, born in Mansfield on 12th September, 1957, has another claim to fame. He is the League's tallest player.

Standing 6ft 5ins in his sky blue Coventry socks, Oggy spearheads the HIGH AND MIGHTY BRIGADE of tall men who stand head and shoulders above their rivals.

There is no more exciting spectacle in First Division action than the sight of an Arsenal corner-kick winging into the Coventry penalty box with

They stand head and shoulders above their rivals

Ogrizovic charging from his line and The Gunners' striker *Niall Quinn* bearing in for the kill.

Quinn is 6ft 4ins.

England defender *Mark Wright* and the Oxford centre-back *Gary Briggs* present a formidable blockade.

They both stand 6ft 3ins high, almost impossible to beat in the air in a straight heading duel.

Mickey Droy, shoring-up the Brentford defence after launching his career at Chelsea before moving to Crystal Palace, is the towering inferno of the Third Division.

Man-mountain Droy is cruising at 10 feet high when he launches his 6ft 4ins frame into space for a clearing header at Griffin Park.

Wakeley Gage, Northampton, Chester and Peterborough, weighs in at 13.06 stone and 6ft 4ins and

STEVE OGRIZOVIC

Mark Wright is almost unbeatable in the air.

Mighty

Arsenal's Niall Quinn rises to the occasion against West Ham.

Charlton, *John Pearson,* stands 6ft 2ins and Gillingham's Republic of Ireland striker Tony Cascarino is the same height.

They're not so hot on the ground but give them the ball above head height and their menace strikes fear into any defence.

And now for something different . . .

Trust Tommy Docherty to come up with an alternative to the High and Mighty Brigade.

Tommy thrust the smallest player in the game into League action when he managed Wolves.

The tiny terror came in the shape of *Paul 'Peewee' Dougherty,* a lad from Leamington measuring just 5ft in height and weighing a bare 8 stone after a big dinner.

Oggy v Peewee . . . now what a contest that would make!

Swindon's former Manchester University forward *Dave Bamber* is no midget at 6ft 3ins.

Dave has worn the colours of Blackpool, Coventry, Walsall, Portsmouth and Swindon in an interesting career of highs and lows.

Who are the other high and mighty performers?

West Ham's goalkeeper *Phil Parkes* rivals Coventry's Oggy by hurling his 6ft 3ins frame around The Hammers' penalty-box.

He joined West Ham for a fee of £450,000, a world record for a goalkeeper at the time.

That staggering transfer fee when he went to Upton Park from QPR meant that John Lyall paid £6,000 per inch of Phil's frame!

Leeds United's capture from

PHIL PARKES

13

Reluctant Hero

Jim Leighton has killed off the myth that Scottish goalkeepers are only good for a giggle on The Saint & Greavsie show.

Poor old Alan Rough returned from the 1982 World Cup Finals with his reputation in tatters but it was a different story for his international successor four years later.

Mexico 1986 was a potential disaster zone for Leighton. Goalkeepers were warned that in the rarefied air, the deadliest free-kick merchants would have the ball swerving and bouncing all over the place.

Leighton, as ever, took it all in his stride. And while the rest of the Scotland team failed to deliver the goods, Jim impressed the watching world with his cool handling and unspectacular style.

Gentleman Jim has gone from strength to strength since then. He has never been a man to hog the headlines, but it is only a matter of time before he passes Rough's record 53 caps for a Scottish 'keeper.

SUPERSONIC SAINT

Southampton ace Colin Clarke is making up for lost time.

He's been a master marksman for a number of years with Tranmere and Bournemouth. But it wasn't until he proved himself in the 1986 World Cup Finals with Northern Ireland that a First Division club were prepared to take a gamble on him.

It was the Saints who stumped up the £400,000 asking price and they've had no cause for complaint.

Sparkling SPINK

Nigel Spink is the best English goalkeeper around – according to his manager, Billy McNeill of Aston Villa – and would make a worthy successor to England 'keeper Peter Shilton when the time comes to replace the international number one.

Nigel makes no secret of the fact he wants to add caps to the one he earned against Australia in 1983 and demonstrates it by putting in a rigorous training schedule similar to the one that has kept Peter Shilton at the top for so long.

''Like me, he's a perfectionist,'' says Nigel. ''But I want that jersey. And I can't wait for English clubs to be allowed back into European competition. Then maybe I'll get the opportunity to add another marvellous memory to the one I savour from that great night in 1982.''

That ''great night'' was when Nigel substituted for an injured Jimmy Rimmer early on in Villa's European Cup Final against Bayern Munich in Rotterdam in 1982 and with a superb series of saves helped his club to an incredible 1–0 victory.

A feat to overshadow that would be starring in a Cup Final for his beloved England!

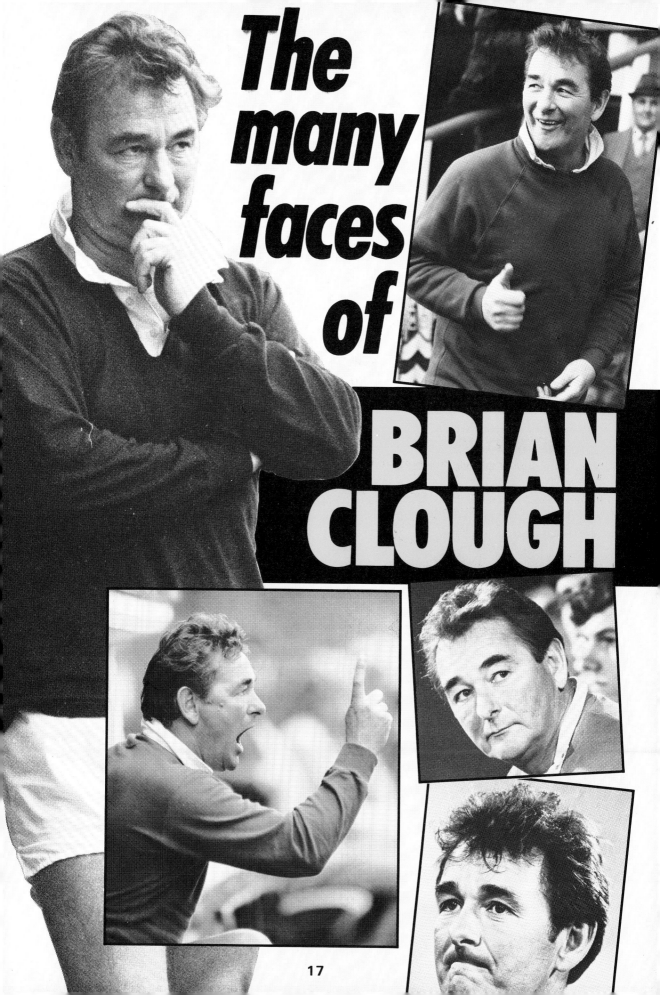

The many faces of BRIAN CLOUGH

It's PUZZLE

Can you identify these three internationals? One is a Parkhead hero, another is gunning for glory and the third is a Danish Red Devil.

HIDDEN STARS

SIGNED UP

Study the autograph and using the clue given can you identify the First Division defender?

He joined The Canaries from Gillingham in 1984?

Answers on page 125

WHAT HAPPENED NEXT?

Study this picture taken during the 1982 FA Cup Replay and describe what happened next.

T1ME

11.

FIND THE STAR

Place the answers to the eleven clues in the corresponding places in the square above. (1 to 10 Across & 11 Down) When this is all completed the letters in the circled squares can be unjumbled to give the name of an Aston Villa defender. (5 & 5)

(1) Gary — , Leicester City player. (10)
(2) John — , Watford defender. (10)
(3) Nigel — , Arsenal defender (right). (10)
(4) Tim — , Luton Town defender. (8)
(5) West Ham defender. (4 & 6)
(6) Arsenal defender. (4 & 5)
(7) Spurs' goalkeeping hero in 1984 UEFA Cup Final (4 & 5)
(8) Manchester City midfielder. (4 & 5)
(9) Paul — , Manchester United defender. (7)
(10) Southampton defender.(5 & 4)
(11) Sheffield Wednesday striker. (3 & 7)

spot the difference

Our artist has made ten alterations to the reproduction. Can you spot them?

Great British triumphs

Steve Chalmers scores Celtic's historic winner against Inter-Milan.

European Cup Final 1967

Celtic 2 Inter-Milan 1

They started the Final in Portugal as Celtic; they finished the game as the "Lisbon Lions".

Celtic's mauling of the great Inter-Milan brought the European Cup to Britain for the first time and the swashbuckling manner in which Billy McNeill, Bobby Murdoch, Bertie Auld, Jimmy Johnstone and the rest destroyed the Italian giants persuaded the rest of Europe to scrap the ultra defensive systems that were beginning to strangle club football.

Tommy Gemmell, Celtic's full back, launched himself into attack to score the first goal and when Chalmers added a second, the 56,000 gate knew that Britain had established a foothold in a tournament that had defeated the best efforts of Football League and Scottish League clubs.

Teams: Celtic — Simpson, Craig, Gemmell, Murdoch, McNeill, Clark, Johnstone, Wallace, Chalmers, Auld, Lennox.

Inter — Sarti, Burgnich, Facchetti, Bedin, Guarneri, Picchi, Bicicli, Mazzola, Cappelini, Corso, Domenghini.

Legend! Sir Matt Busby congratulates Alex Stepney after Manchester United's great night at Wembley.

European Cup Final 1968

Manchester Utd 4 Benfica 1

Five goals, a breathtakingly emotional climax to Matt Busby's managerial reign, but Manchester United's goalkeeper Alex Stepney stole much of the glory from his team-mates with a wonder save.

The teams were locked at 1–1 after Bobby Charlton's brilliant headed goal had been cancelled out by Graca's equaliser.

Now, Eusebio, the 'Eagle of Lisbon' was bearing down on the United goal in search of the winner for Benfica. He unleashed a ferocious shot but Stepney, moving like lightning, made a staggering save to force extra-time.

Stepney's magic became the turning point in United's fortunes. George Best put United ahead after a jinking run through Benfica's spreadeagled ranks; Brian Kidd, celebrating his 19th birthday, made it 3–1 after heading against the crossbar, and Bobby Charlton cracked the fourth just before the final whistle.

Teams: Manchester Utd — Stepney, Brennan, Dunne, Crerand, Foulkes, Stiles, Best, Kidd, Charlton, Sadler, Aston.

Benfica — Henrique, Adolfo, Humberto, Jacinto, Cruz, Graca, Coluna, Augusto, Eusebio, Torres, Simoes.

GLORY DAYS

in Europe

Penalty! Kevin Keegan is scythed down by Berti Vogts. Phil Neal scored from the spot to ensure Liverpool of their first European Cup success.

European Cup Final 1977

Liverpool 3 Bor. M'gladbach 1

Terry McDermott set mighty Liverpool on the path to a famous victory in their 13th successive season in European competition with a superbly constructed goal in Rome on May 25.

He worked his magic in the 27th minute, taking Steve Heighway's diagonal pass in his stride before stroking it first time into the net.

Jimmy Case's mistake let in Allan Simonsen for an equaliser, but that man Heighway popped up again to spring a corner into Borussia's penalty area for

Tommy Smith — playing because of injury to Phil Thompson — to head Liverpool into the lead.

Now, Kevin Keegan took over, bursting beyond his 'shadow' Berti Vogts only for the West German to scythe him down in the penalty-area.

Phil Neal made no mistake with the spot-kick — and Emlyn Hughes raised the trophy to the 57,000 crowd.

It was the best final for years.

Teams: Liverpool — Clemence, Neal, Jones, Smith, Kennedy, Hughes, Keegan, Case, Heighway, Callaghan, McDermott.

Borussia — Kneib, Vogts, Klinkhammer, Wittkampf, Bonhof, Wohlers (Hannes), Simonsen, Wimmer (Kulik), Stielike, Schaffer, Heynckes.

European Cup Final 1978

Liverpool 1 Bruges 0

Liverpool's two big signings, Kenny Dalglish and Graeme Souness, produced one of the few flashes of inspiration in a disappointing Final at Wembley to set up the Reds' second successive triumph in the competition.

The decisive moment arrived in the 65th minute when Dalglish produced a spark of genius that was to become a feature of his playing career at Anfield.

Souness, transferred from Middlesbrough, sent a searching ball to fellow Scot Dalglish on the right of the penalty area.

Dalglish outflanked a defender in a race to the six yard area and as Jensen committed himself to a dive, Dalglish coolly chipped the ball over the advancing goalkeeper's body.

Liverpool had become the first British side to win the Cup twice — and 92,000 fans acknowledged their triumph in a rousing salute.

Teams: Liverpool — Clemence, Neal, Hughes, Thompson, Kennedy R, Hansen, Dalglish, Case (Heighway), Fairclough,

Liverpool retained the European Cup in 1978 thanks to Kenny Dalglish.

CONTINUED OVERLEAF

OUR GLORY, GLORY DAYS

CONTINUED FROM P21

McDermott, Souness.

Bruges — Jensen, Bastijns, Maes (Volder), Krieger, Leekens, Cools, De Cubber, Vandereycken, Simoen, Ku (Sanders), Sorensen.

European Cup Final 1981

Liverpool 1 Real Madrid 0

Alan Kennedy scored one of the best goals seen in a Euro Final when he lashed the ball into Real's net with only eight minutes remaining of a tightly fought game in Paris.

Both teams were desperate to win. Real, who won the first five European Cup competitions, had not won since their record sixth win in 1966.

Liverpool had won twice, and wanted to join those clubs, Bayern Munich and Ajax, who had won the Cup three times.

Juanito and Laurie Cunningham, the England star playing in Spain, produced flashes of skill in the first half and Santillana twice came close to scoring.

But Alan Kennedy mastered Cunningham in the second half and had the enterprise to take a Ray Kennedy throw-in on his chest before sweeping into Real's penalty area to unleash a shot of stunning power beyond the startled Agustin.

Teams: Liverpool — Clemence, Neal, Thompson, Hansen, Kennedy A, Lee, McDermott, Souness, Kennedy R, Dalglish (Case), Johnson.

Real Madrid — Agustin, Garcia Cortes (Pineda), Garcia Navajas, Sabido, Del Bosque, Angel, Camacho, Stielike, Juanito, Santillana, Cunningham.

Real Madrid's England star Laurie Cunningham showed flashes of brilliance against Liverpool.

European Cup Winners' Cup Final 1985

Everton 3 Rapid Vienna 1

Andy Gray has maintained always that he scored two goals in Everton's first triumph in Europe.

The Scottish international striker remains convinced that he opened the scoring in Rotterdam with a close range shot.

The linesman signalled Mountfield off-side but subsequent video replays suggest the referee made a mistake.

But Gray was not to be denied his moment of glory in the second half when Graeme Sharp seized on a bad back pass, went past 'keeper Konsel to the by-line and presented Gray with a gift chance.

The veteran Panenka came on to grab the initiative from Everton but the Merseysiders soon recovered their composure for Trevor Steven to thump Sheedy's corner into Rapid's net.

Krankl, well held by Mountfield and Kevin Ratcliffe, scored 10 minutes from time but Rapid's joy was short-lived when Sharp sent Sheedy bounding through Rapid's defence to hammer a 20 yarder past a bewildered Konsel.

Teams: Everton — Southall, Stevens, van den Hauwe, Ratcliffe, Mountfield, Reid, Steven, Sharp, Gray, Bracewell, Sheedy.

Rapid Vienna — Konsel, Lainer, Brauneder, Weber, Garger, Kranjcar, Kienast, Hrstick, Pacult (Groess), Krankl, Weinhofer (Panenka).

Hero! Two-goal Andy Gray (far right) helped Everton to their first European triumph in 1985.

It all looked serious enough as Trevor Peake and Clive Allen clashed in last season's FA Cup Final but . . .

Clive takes off

. . . the pair had secretly been practising a dance routine and showed off their new act in front of the 98,000 Wembley crowd.

When Alan Cork popped up with a goal against Leicester City early last season it was his first in Division One and the 118th of his League career with Wimbledon.

But it also completed a personal record of scoring in all four Divisions as follows:

Division 4	1977–78	4
	1978–79	22
	1980–81	23
	1982–83	5
Division 3	1979–80	12
	1981–82	nil
	1983–84	29
	(club record)	
Division 2	1984–85	11
	1985–86	11
Division 1	1986–87	7

He now holds three records at Wimbledon: most goals in a season, highest aggregate of goals and more League appearances than any other Dons player.

But for injury which at one time threatened to end his

1979.

And although goalscoring overall has tended to fall away in recent years, there have been a number of outstanding feats of late, notably a most unique 'double' in the League three seasons ago.

On two separate days, two different players each scored five times. The first occasion was on September 10, 1983 when *Simon Garner* scored all five for Blackburn Rovers in a 5–1 win over Derby County and *Tony Caldwell* hit five himself in Bolton Wanderers 8–1 victory against Walsall.

Incredibly the following month on October 29, *Tony Woodcock* scored five of Arsenal's goals in their 6–2 win at Aston Villa, while *Ian Rush* matched it with five in

GOLDEN

Great goalscoring feats that had the fans roaring . . .

career, Alan would have added considerably to his overall total of goals and games. His best individual performance in the League was scoring four goals in a Division Four game against Torquay United on 28 February,

Alan Brazil (number 10) scored all five goals for Ipswich against Southampton in February, 1982.

Liverpool's 6–0 success over Luton Town.

Of course, players scoring all or most of a high scoring team's goals is still fairly common. Last season *Clive Allen* scored more than half of Tottenham's

League total for the season. Before then *Ted MacDougall* produced 42 of Bournemouth's 81 Fourth Division goals in 1970–71.

The following season he established an FA Cup record

24

Ian Rush scores the second of his five goals in a 6–0 rout of Luton Town.

Aldershot v Halifax, May, 1983.

It is not common for a player to have had as many as three separate spells with one League club, but Chesterfield's *Ernie Moss* made it a scoring experience on each occasion.

At the end of the 1985–86 season he had taken his total in three spells with the team to 153 League goals while other service with Peterborough, Mansfield, Port Vale, Lincoln and Doncaster produced a further 70 to give him 223 overall.

Kenny Dalglish is not the only goalscorer to hit a century of goals on either side of the border but he is the latest and the most famous.

In Celtic's colours he achieved 112 League goals and at the end of 1985–86 he had scored exactly the same number for Liverpool.

SHOTS

with nine goals for Bournemouth in a tie against Margate.

A much travelled striker his lengthy career took him later to Manchester United, West Ham United, Norwich City, Southampton, Bournemouth (again) and Blackpool.

MacDougall, who won seven caps for Scotland, scored 256 League goals, reaching his 250th for Bournemouth against Rochdale in November 1979.

Hat-tricks of penalty-kicks have been rare but not unknown. *Trevor Anderson* did it for Swindon Town v Walsall in April 1976, *Alan Slough* Peterborough United v Chester two years later and *Andy Blair* Sheffield Wednesday v Luton Town in a Milk Cup game in November 1984.

Other recent five goal men in the League have featured *Roger Davies* Derby County v Luton Town on March 29, 1975; *Alan Brazil* Ipswich Town v Southampton on February 16, 1982 and *Dale Banton*

Wimbledon's Alan Cork heads home his first goal in Division One against Leicester City at Plough Lane.

IDENTI-FIT

There are three clues to the identity of each player. Maximum points if you get him in one — minimum if it takes you three shots!

15 points
10 points
5 points

(These values to be set against the three clues to each player.)

1 A striker, he's Nottingham-born and joined his club from Long Eaton United.

2 Won a League Cup winner's medal in 1979, scoring two goals at Wembley. An England international, first capped in 1980 v Argentina.

3 Sold to Manchester United for £1,250,000. Bought back in 1982.

1 Jamaican-born, this black striker joined his club from a non-League team.

2 Top scorer for his club at the end of season 1984—85 with 28 goals overall. England international, first capped in 1983 v West Germany.

3 Sold to Italian club AC Milan for £1 million. Later returned to his club for half that figure.

1 Born in Glasgow, this great defender joined his club from Eastercraigs in 1971. Now their very successful captain.

2 A Scottish international, he was first capped v Russia in 1975. Is his club's most capped player.

3 Winner of many trophies, including a European Cup-Winners' Cup winner's medal. Has played well over 400 League games for his club.

ANSWERS ON PAGE 125

LEEDS LEADER

Ian Baird climbs above the QPR defence to head Leeds United into the lead in a Fifth Round F.A. Cup-tie last season.

CRAZY CAPERS

W ho said the fun has gone out of football? Cricket, rugby, tennis, athletics, darts and snooker might take life a bit seriously, but there's plenty to bring a smile to the face of football.

Grrr, what a pair of pins

Help mate — Glenn Hoddle gets a lift from BBCTV's John Motson.

Spanish clown

Let's face it — Gary Lineker.

Supersub Nigel

Early Clough and Son — a very young Nigel gives SHOOT a smile.

For my next trick

Well-balanced player — Alan Devonshire.

Caked

Mudlark — Ossie Ardiles.

Spitting Shiltage

Model 'keeper — Peter Shilton with his Madam Tussaud's waxwork.

No Spurs please — Ray Clemence takes top jockey Steve Smith-Eccles for a ride.

Ray's a Laugh

FOOTBALL FUNNIES

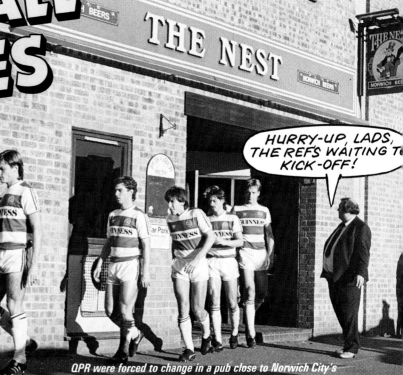

"The boss is very religious, especially when it comes to last minute penalties in F.A. Cup Semi-Finals."

QPR were forced to change in a pub close to Norwich City's Carrow Road a couple of years ago because of a fire that destroyed the main stand.

"I hope Chelsea won't mind us calling ourselves 'The Pensioners'"

I'M GLAD IT'S HALF-TIME, I CAN DO WITH 40 WINKS

Liverpool's Craig Johnston shows signs of fatigue during a close-season game abroad.

"But it was his fault, ref. He tripped me up!"

CLUB TROPHY CABINET

"The chairman won it in a knobbly knees competition at Butlins."

John McClelland is the man who missed out on the boom times at Glasgow Rangers.

Amazing as it might seem considering Rangers have splashed more than £2 million in their bid to revive the glory days at Ibrox, McClelland quit — *because the club wouldn't make him a good enough financial offer!*

That sounds rich to the Northern Ireland international and former Rangers skipper, when he looks back to his days at Ibrox compared to more recent times.

Graeme Souness' expensive recruiting campaign has netted so

MEAN RANGERS!

Why John McClelland quit Ibrox for Watford

many top stars, principally from English clubs, that money has been flowing out of the Rangers coffers.

McClelland moved to Watford to find the financial security he wanted. But he says: ''I don't hold any grudges against Rangers. In fact I'm absolutely delighted for all their marvellous fans that the club has at last realised its great potential.

''There is no reason why they could not enjoy the sort of success Liverpool have had in European football. The potential at that club is phenomenal.''

McClelland always knew that during his three-and-a-half years there, most of them as captain.

''The supporters were magnificent all the time I was there even though we didn't have real success. I think we reached five Cup Finals in that time and won two, lost three of them.''

McClelland believes Souness will now seek to develop the junior levels of the club, so that Rangers can find and teach their own stars of the future.

It would be easy for the big Watford defender to look back and think what might have been if he had stayed North of the border.

''When I left, it was highlighted about terms at Rangers,'' he says. ''Yet I agreed terms within five minutes at Watford. And with the best will in the world, Watford cannot compare in size with a club like Glasgow Rangers. So something was clearly wrong.''

McClelland negotiated for nine months about a new deal before finally losing patience and leaving Rangers. He said: ''I offered to sign for the rest of my career. I never wanted to go. I just wanted a decent wage for a decent job — a top wage which I felt I was worth.

''I had not been in for a wage rise for three years yet I'd played in the World Cup Finals and earned lots of caps for Northern Ireland. Yet the club just didn't seem to want to come up with the right sort of offer and it became inevitable I would have to go.''

McClelland was lucky — he couldn't have found a nicer club than Watford, nor as honest and ambitious a manager to work for as Graham Taylor. His commitment to the Watford cause is not questioned but he can be forgiven for a wistful look back at the times of growing success for his old club.

''The fans of Ibrox have been patient for so long they deserve all the glories that should come their way over the next few years,'' says John.

31

Ken Brown once sold Dave Watson and Chris Woods for £1.5m, signed their replacements for little over £200,000, and guided Norwich to the top of the First Division all within the space of three months.

Rarely, though, will shrewd wheeler-dealer Brown complete a more rewarding transaction than the time he paid Grimsby £105,000 for Kevin Drinkell.

Granted Brown and Norwich were aided by an independent tri-

people wondered whether he had what it takes to make an impact in the First.

"But I think he proved in less than six months that he was up to it.

"The main thing that strikes me about Kevin is his strength and the way he puts it to use.

"I'll guarantee that when one of our lads puts a cross into the box Kevin will either be on the end of it or close by, because he's as brave as a lion.

"He'll gladly stick his head where others wouldn't put their foot.

"He also possesses good ball control and quite a bit of speed. You don't need much more to be a top class striker."

And Bruce doesn't doubt that Drinkell is among the First Division's top strikers. He adds: "There is an elite bunch of British strikers including Gary Lineker, Ian Rush and Clive Allen.

"Then you have a collection of

NORWICH TO DRINKELL

bunal who set the fee in June 1985, but as Brown points out: "We were taking a gamble because although Drinkell had a fairly good goals record it had been achieved in the lower divisions. He was untried at the top level."

Drinkell – valued by Grimsby at three times that fee – has since used his muscular 5ft 11ins frame to shove aside any doubts about his ability.

In his first season at Carrow Road Drinkell netted 22 goals as Norwich romped to the Second Division Championship and last season did more than enough to help consolidate Norwich's position in the top flight.

Not surprisingly Brown is delighted with his investment. He says: "Kevin had a good apprenticeship at Grimsby. He could have been a flop after joining us but he has worked hard at his game and has been absolutely brilliant for us."

Norwich skipper Steve Bruce adds: "Kevin is similar to me in as much as he spent his formative years in the lower divisions, and

Norwich skipper Steve Bruce, resisting this challenge from Wimbledon's John Fashanu, rates team-mate Drinkell among the top strikers in the First Division.

what I would call quality strikers including Tony Cottee, Frank McAvennie and Graeme Sharp. I would certainly place Kevin among that lot.''

No wonder Grimsby are still smarting. They could have sold Drinkell to Middlesbrough for a hefty £350,000 when he was just 19, but held onto him until he'd scored 89 goals in 270 League appearances.

Drinkell recalls: ''Various clubs showed regular interest in me, but Grimsby always seemed to want more money than was being offered.

''Turning down Middlesbrough's £350,000 for example certainly backfired on them.''

Drinkell's wish to play at a higher level was realised only when his contract at Blundell Park had expired.

''I refused to sign a new contract,'' he remembers, ''and Norwich were in contact almost immediately.

''I travelled to Norwich to speak to Ken Brown and signed practically there and then because, although they had just been relegated to the Second Division, I was sure that with the squad they had they'd soon be back in Division One. I was proved right!''

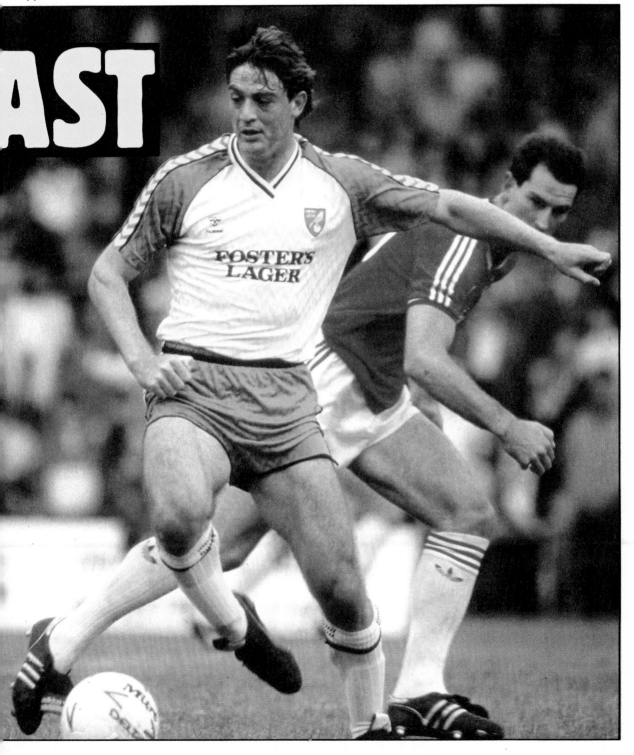

Sheffield Wednesday striker Lee Chapman recalls his

ARSENAL AGONY!

Lee Chapman believes George Graham has put the smile back on the face of Arsenal football for one major reason — his tough line in discipline.

And the big Sheffield Wednesday striker should know — for he spent an unhappy period of his career at Highbury in the days when glory was very far from The Gunners.

Chapman says: ''I am not surprised Arsenal improved so much last season. The fact is, they had to do it sooner or later. I have a lot of respect for the club because they are, one of the biggest and most glamorous in the world.''

Chapman went to Arsenal in a blaze of publicity over his £500,000 transfer from Stoke City.

It looked like a dream move for the former Stoke lad but became a nightmare which was resolved only when Chapman left and headed back up North.

''The big difference between Arsenal now and in those days is just one word — discipline,'' he says. ''George Graham has put it on the line both on and off the field.

''From what I hear, he started off the field and it has carried on during games.

''There was not anything like as much discipline when I was there and the Arsenal club did not have the same sense of purpose at that time.

''It was a pity because it was an enormous disappointment for me not to make it there and succeed. But these things happen in life and you have to accept them.''

Chapman believes the

experience, although painful at the time, was of long term benefit to him.

''I learned a lot about myself which was good for me. Of course, if I'd had the choice, I would not have gone through those times because they were very difficult. But you only learn about yourself when things don't go right.''

Now Sheffield Wednesday could be set to follow the example of Arsenal and begin to restore better times.

''We are at the crossroads really, capable of success in all the competitions, but not quite consistent enough so far.

''But like Arsenal, the support is tremendous at this club and I would say it is probably more intense than it was at Highbury.

''The pressure is there in a different way and the fans here are more keen for us to do well.

''It is still a big club, lovely stadium and the support is there. Everything is geared for success.''

PAUL'S BROUGHT BLUES A POWER OF GOOD

When most First Division players of 30-plus are starting to think about past glories and stepping down into a less-demanding Division or hanging up their boots, Paul Power took on the challenge of fighting for a place at a new club thrusting for the top honours.

Veteran Paul, with 11 years and 365 League games behind him at Manchester City, accepted an offer from Everton manager Howard Kendall to join the Goodison Park club in the summer of 1986. Originally the plan was for Paul to act as cover for established Blues' stars, but the opportunity came for him to step into the first team at the start of the 1986-87 season through an injury to Pat Van den Hauwe and Paul certainly made the most of it.

Speed

At the age of 33, he showed that he still combined skill and experience with a turn of speed that surprised opponents and Everton fans, too.

"I've always put great emphasis on keeping as fit as possible," he says. "At City my position was at full-back, and when I moved to Everton I was fairly confident I could cope. But moving up to midfield, where you're on the go all the game, was something I had doubts about. So I've been delighted at how well I coped in that department, even getting on the scoresheet at times.

"Everton gave me a two-year contract. If things go well, they can turn out to be the best years of my footballing life."

Rampant Regis

Coventry boss George Curtis has no doubts. ''When he's on top of his form, there is no better striker in England than Cyrille Regis.''

But Curtis is also aware that his muscular centre-forward reaches those peaks all too rarely.

Inconsistency has been Regis' greatest handicap throughout a career which has never reached the heights which many people eagerly anticipated when he first broke into the West Bromwich Albion team under Ron Atkinson.

A £300,000 transfer to Coventry in October, 1984, failed to revive his career, and it wasn't until Curtis and his chief coach John Sillett took charge at Highfield Road that big Cyrille took off again.

''The credit is down to Sillett,'' says Curtis. ''Instead of whacking long balls up to him, John made Cyrille the big cog in our wheel and played the ball to his feet.''

The transformation has been remarkable. ''I'm playing my best football for years,'' says Cyrille.

''But Coventry's revival is not solely down to me. The whole team has played well and that has helped us shrug off the inferiority complex we had.''

Mick's a taker

Few players in recent years have given better value for money than Portsmouth's £150,000 striker Mick Quinn.

Yet there was a stage in the Liverpudlian's career when it seemed he would never make it to the top of his profession.

His first club, Derby County, let him go without a first team chance, and even when he started to make a

name for himself in the lower divisions with Wigan, no top club was prepared to take a gamble on him.

Luckily for Mick, Oldham boss Joe Royle realised his potential and it remains one of his biggest regrets that financial difficulties forced him to release Quinn to his old mate Alan Ball at such a knockdown price.

Within a year of his arrival at Fratton Park, Mick had already paid off his fee with 27 priceless goals.

Mo Johnston
SCOTLAND

Dozzell's super-sharp

The Jason Dozzell you see now grafting non-stop in midfield for Ipswich Town is far faster and has greater staying power than the one who played two seasons ago in the club's relegation season. Who says so? None other than Jason himself.

"In some games at that time I tended to run out of steam and act a bit slow. I realised I needed to sharpen my reflexes and to work up my stamina. It certainly paid off last term."

What Jason doesn't say in his defence, though, is that he's still a maturing teenager and then he was very much a boy in a man's world.

Jason exploded into soccer's headlines around three years ago when he scored the debut goal against Coventry City that made him the First Division's youngest-ever marksman at 16 and 57 days. And he was still a schoolboy.

Jason's growing up fast. There's still plenty of time to add that full England cap to his collection of Youth ones.

Fearless Fash

John Fashanu admits he will never be the most skilful centre-forward in the world.

But his awesome physical presence and fearless appetite for a scrap would win him a place in most managers' starting line-up.

"I feel as though I've been the distance with Frank Bruno," complained Steve Bruce after one particularly bruising encounter with the muscular former Barnardo boy.

But Fashanu is quick to play down the controversy which has surrounded his style ever since he first made his mark in the First Division with Wimbledon.

"I get labelled a hard-man because I tend to ignore all defenders in my determination to get that ball," he says.

"But I am not as mean as I am made out to be and I don't think any defender can accuse me of being unfair.

"What they will confirm is that they have been in a hard game.

"Football is a physical sport and I take far more knocks than I ever dish out."

Forest's *fast* Learner

It takes more than just a hatful of goals to satisfy Brian Clough.

Even a strike rate better than any other midfield man in the country has not been enough to keep Neil Webb in the Forest boss' good books.

"We know he will always score goals, but there are other aspects of his trade which Webb still has to learn," says Clough.

And the former Reading and Portsmouth star agrees.

"I'm the kind of player who needs a rocket from time to time, and you can be certain that the boss obliges me on that score," laughs Webb.

Lev Yashin in World Cup action during the 1966 Finals in England.

EURO

*The European Championship draws to a thrilling climax at the Finals in West Germany next summer.
England will be striving to win their first European Championship title since the tournament was launched 28 years ago.*

Lev Yashin
GOALKEEPER

RUSSIA 2, Yugoslavia 1 (a.e.t.)

1960 Paris

The Man in Black – he was always black jerseyed – Yashin shored-up Russia's defence in their 2-1 victory in extra time over Yugoslavia in Paris.

No Yugoslav player managed to beat him in the 1960 Final. The goal he conceded swept past him from Netto, one of his own players.

But goals from Metreveli and the winner from Ponedelnik gave Russia their only European Championship trophy, won in that first tournament.

Yashin, tall and spectacular, is the most famous player ever to come out of Russia. He played in three World Cups, and first won the hearts of British fans for his magnificent display in goal for the Rest of the World against England at Wembley in 1963.

Born in Moscow in 1929, Yashin was a natural athlete. He left school at 14, worked in an aircraft factory, and in his spare time played ice-hockey, basketball, volleyball, swam and dived, and impressed at athletics.

Fortunately he bacame a footballer, winning all his caps as a Moscow Dynamo player. He stayed with Dynamo as a coach after his retirement.

Luis Suarez
MIDFIELD

SPAIN 2, Russia 1

1964 Madrid

Suarez became the world's first £200,000 player when he left Barcelona for Internazionale (Milan) in 1962 but all his Italian connections were forgotten two years later in Madrid when his midfield brilliance helped destroy a powerful Russian team in the 1964 European Championship Final.

Suarez was arguably Europe's best midfielder in the 1960s. Born in La Coruna on May 2, 1935, his vision, pace and incredible body swerve persuaded Barcelona to snap him up when he was only 18.

He won his first cap for Spain in 1957 and was an established star when he helped Barcelona reach the 1961 European Cup Final.

His power and control steered Spain to the 1962 World Cup Finals in Chile and he went on to star for Internazionale in their European Cup Final triumphs of 1964 v. Real Madrid and 1965 v. Benfica.

Sandro Mazzola
STRIKER

ITALY 2, Yugoslavia 0

1968 ROME

Mazzola masterminded Italy's handsome victory over Yugoslavia in a 1968 Final replay in Rome from his new position in midfield.

Riva and Anastasi, the new strike-force, dealt the hammer blows but Mazzola's stealth helped set up Italy's only win in the tournament.

Mazzola was an exception to the rule that sons rarely emulate the talents of their famous fathers in football.

Son of Valentino Mazzola, who was killed with his Torino team-mates in a 'plane crash in 1949, Sandro developed his brilliant goal-scoring skills with Internazionale boys team in Milan.

Quicksilver inside the penalty box with an unerring eye for a half chance, Mazzola played in three World Cups, scoring on the first of 70 appearances for Italy against Brazil in May 1963.

His brilliance was unstoppable as he spearheaded Inter's wins in two European Cups, in 1964 and 1965.

Left: Gerd Muller on target for West Germany. Below: Rummenigge knew he would score.

MAGIC!

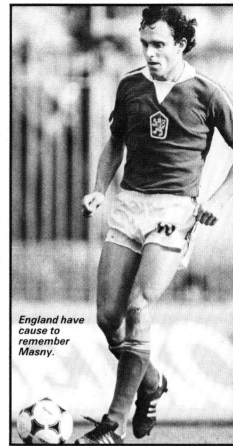
England have cause to remember Masny.

While England have nothing to celebrate in several unsuccessful attempts to impose themselves on the tournament, others have used the Finals as a platform for their breathtaking skills. This is a tribute to the heroes of past Finals whose records have earned them a place in history.

Gerd Muller **STRIKER**	Mario Masny **MIDFIELD**	Karl-Heinz Rummenigge **STRIKER**
W. GERMANY 3, Russia 0	CZECH. 2, Germany 2 (a.e.t.) Czechs won 5-3 on penalties	W. GERMANY 2, Belgium 1
1972 Brussels	**1976 Belgrade**	**1980 ROME**

1972 Brussels

Muller became one of the world's deadliest goal-machines in an astonishing career for West Germany.

His double-strike against Russia in the 1972 European Championship Final in Brussels helped the Germans establish a clear supremacy over all other European nations in the tournament.

Muller scored 69 goals in 62 games for West Germany, and cracked the 300 mark for Bayern Munich in the Bundesliga.

His last goal for West Germany was that which won the 1974 World Cup Final.

Englishmen will never forget that left foot volley that sent Alf Ramsey's team crashing out of the World Cup at Leon in 1970.

Squat, dark, and heavily muscled in the Maradona-mould, he has never received the credit he deserved for his goal-scoring exploits, which far outstrip Jimmy Greaves' record for England.

1976 Belgrade

Masny's incredible skills on the ball earned him a 'George Best' tag in the 1970s.

His talents were never better displayed than in the European Championship tournament, decided after two years of action, in Belgrade.

The German's were at their best in this period after winning the World Cup in 1974 and the European Championship in 1972, but Masny and Czechoslovakia were equal to their task in a cliff-hanging penalty shoot-out to decide the 1976 Final.

Masny did more than anyone to see Czechoslovakia into the Finals. His goals in the qualifying rounds helped sink Cyprus twice and England have good cause to remember the little imp for his stunning performance against them in a 2-1 Czech victory in Bratislava on October 30, 1975.

That defeat killed off England's hopes of qualifying.

1980 ROME

A group of photographers have never forgotten Kalle's astounding prediction in the European Championship Final against Belgium.

With the scores level, and seconds on the clock, West Germany won a corner which Rummenigge took. He ran past a phalanx of photographers, winking at them as he passed, and telling them: "There's a goal coming up."

Sure enough, the ball curled menacingly from the impish striker's foot onto the head of Horst Hrubesch . . . and Belgium were dead.

Born on 29th September, 1955, he has twice won the coveted European Footballer of the year title after springing to prominence in the 1978 World Cup Finals and the 1980 European Championships.

Injury blunted his razor-sharp skills in the 1982 World Cup in Spain, and by the 1986 Finals in Mexico he was a shadow of the player at his best.

MITCHELL EARNS

HIS SPURS

David Pleat's first priority when he took charge at Tottenham last year was to overhaul the club's all too brittle defence.

So it was no surprise when, within weeks of arriving at White Hart Lane, he went back to his former club, Luton, to sign their promising young defender Mitchell Thomas.

It was a deal which left The Hatters seething, but Thomas shrugged off the controversy to instantly win over the Spurs fans with a series of outstanding performances at left-back.

England boss Bobby Robson soon recognised Thomas' potential and now the Luton-born defender is the regular understudy to the reliable Kenny Sansom.

But Thomas is quick to give praise to Spurs skipper Richard Gough for his instant success at White Hart Lane.

''Richard arrived at the club at about the same time as me, but because he'd cost £750,000 and my fee was only a third of that, there was a lot more pressure on him to do well,'' reveals Thomas.

''But Richard handled it all so casually that he inspired me to do the same.

''He spreads confidence throughout the defence and has helped me no end with his calls. It was no surprise that the boss made him captain within four months.''

Now Mitchell's goal is to become a regular England player.

*A*nyone who believes that Terry Butcher has lowered his standards to play in the Scottish Premier Division for Rangers gets short shrift from the brilliant England defender. ''You've got to be good to survive up here,'' he says. ''The game is played at such a ferocious pace that defenders don't have time to dwell on the ball. There is always someone snapping at my heels, and as a result my distribution has actually improved.''

McInally's debt to Clough

Jim McInally was once rated a fifth choice left-back by first club Celtic.

But the Dundee United star's travels across the border and back again have forced Parkhead boss Davie Hay to eat his words.

McInally's stay in England was a brief one. But in his first season with Nottingham Forest he scooped their Player of the Year award.

Brian Clough paid Celtic a mere £40,000 for McInally and doubled his money 15 months later when he sold him to Coventry.

Being sent to Coventry proved something of a nightmare for the 23-year-old who now operates in midfield. After just five senior outings for The Sky Blues he jumped at the chance to return to Scotland.

It was a case of second time lucky for Dundee United manager Jim McLean who also snapped up former Hearts midfield man Davie Bowman in a £140,000 double deal.

He'd tried, without success, to sign McInally from Celtic after the youngster had impressed in a loan spell across the road at Dundee.

''I didn't have to think twice when United came in for me,'' recalls McInally.

''It was also something of a relief to get away from Coventry. Things went wrong there right from the start when I wrote off my car in a crash on my way to my very first training session,

''Then I was unlucky enough to pick up a hamstring injury and was out for a month. Eventually, George Curtis took over from Donald Mackay and I found myself in the reserves.''

It was quite a contrast to his spell with Forest. ''I thoroughly enjoyed working with Brian Clough,'' he says. ''He is definitely one of a kind and it was an experience I wouldn't have missed.''

OH, BROTHERS!

Brian and Mark Stein are a rarity in the game these days. Brothers playing for the same club. In the colours of Luton Town they form an attacking double-act that has earned the respect of First Division opponents, with Brian working down the middle and Mark on the wing mainly supplying crosses.

They hail from a footballing family of seven brothers. In age, Brian is number three and Mark is number seven, the youngest.

Brian was bought by Luton from a non-League club for a measly £2,000, while Mark is a product of the government youth training scheme.

Both of them are fast, tricky and hard to handle – especially on the controversial plastic Kenilworth Road pitch.

Brian has one England cap, against France. His performance was below par and he longs to get the chance to rectify it and show what he really can do.

Mark burst into The Hatters' side last season, scoring five goals in five games at one stage, but while Brian is an established first-team player, Mark has to fight hard for his place.

Mark Stein takes on Arsenal and England full-back Kenny Sansom.

ACE OF HEARTS

TENACIOUS little John Colquhoun winces when someone calls him a wide-boy.

''People thought I was a winger when I first signed for Celtic a few years ago,'' says the Hearts raider.

''Celts had the likes of Frank McGarvey, Mo Johnston and Brian McClair playing through the middle and I was simply pushed wide.''

However, Colquhoun's striking talents were immediately in evidence when Celtic sold him to Hearts for £60,000 three seasons ago and Tynecastle supremo Alex MacDonald put him in his three-pronged strike-force along with John Robertson and Sandy Clark.

''That was the way I had played at Stirling Albion to attract Celtic in the first place and then my style was changed at Parkhead.''

Colquhoun got the spectacular goal for Hearts in their Scottish Cup Semi-Final triumph over Dundee United at Hampden two seasons ago, but fortune didn't favour the brave on the run-in to the campaign.

Hearts had gone over 30 games without defeat and had led the League for most of the season. However, on the last day of the League programme they were shocked 2—0 at Dundee while Colquhoun's old mates at Parkhead conquered St. Mirren 5—0 to claim the Championship on goal difference.

A week later Hearts and Colquhoun met Aberdeen in the Scottish Cup Final and crashed 3—0.

''It was a real choker,'' admits the Tynecastle livewire. ''But the foundation was laid that season for better things to come.''

MARK HUGHES
WALES

ENGLAND'S FORGOTTEN

DAVID ARMSTRONG

Still good enough

Southampton's David Armstrong (below) has not given up hope of an international recall.

"I still think I am good enough to play at the highest level," he says, "and I have a scoring record that is second to none for a midfield player, with a goal in every three or four games.

"All the same I have no argument with the team selection. The decision must always be with the manager and, of course, I have paid a price because Bryan Robson has been such a great influence on the side."

Armstrong played three times for England between 1980 and 1984.

DEREK STATHAM

A good run

Kenny Sansom has been a fixture in the England side for so long it is hard to remember that at one time many judges thought West Brom's Derek Statham (above) was a better left-back.

Statham did force his way into the side for three caps in 1983, but he was then hit by injuries. With Albion struggling in the League as well, he has been out of the reckoning.

The unlucky Statham hasn't given up all hope of returning to the England team.

"I don't see why I can't get back. It's just a question of putting together the performances," says the 27-year-old.

BRIAN STEIN

50

MEN

Players recall their brief, but sometimes memorable international careers . . .

Too many strikers

"I just wish I'd had an easier game," says Luton's Brian Stein (below), recalling his one England appearance against France in 1984. "They were the best side in the world at the time. It's a shame we didn't play someone like Turkey.

"In retrospect, I feel that both Paul Walsh and I should have had another shout, but you can't pick and choose your games. I had the opportunity."

The Luton striker hasn't given up hope of another one, though. "You try to do the best to your ability, but there's a lot of strikers about at the moment," he added.

JOHN GREGORY
Bizarre debut

Derby County's John Gregory (below), who won six caps in 1983–84, doesn't expect to receive his country's call again—but then he was amazed to be chosen in the first place.

"I was 29-years-old and after playing in the First Division for six years I thought my chance had gone," he confessed. "But it tasted that much sweeter when it came."

Then with QPR, Gregory won his first cap in Australia. "It was a bizarre debut," he recalls. "But to change in the same dressing room as Len Hutton, Colin Cowdrey and Geoff Boycott made it doubly memorable."

PETER DAVENPORT
A bonus

Manchester United striker Peter Davenport (above) has just one solitary England cap to his name, and that as a substitute. But in the 20 minutes he was on the Wembley pitch he made a vital contribution to England's World Cup campaign.

It was he that set up Gary Lineker's first goal for England in that match against the Republic of Ireland and the Barcelona ace hasn't stopped scoring since.

In contrast Davenport struggled with injury and then loss of form following his transfer from Nottingham Forest.

"At the moment I'm just getting my head down for Manchester United, anything else would be a bonus," said Davenport.

51

Maradona for Tottenham!

What's the world's greatest star Diego Maradona doing playing for Spurs? It's not trick photography. Diego guested for Tottenham in Ossie Ardiles' Testimonial game against Inter-Milan at White Hart Lane last year. Spurs won.

Gregory's gamble pays off

John Gregory isn't a gambling man by nature. But he backed himself to succeed on odds of 70-30 the day he joined struggling Derby County in the Third Division.

His gamble looks like paying off handsomely for the player who was an experienced First Division man with a trio of clubs, Aston Villa, Brighton and Queens Park Rangers.

Gregory got the chance to go North, from QPR, when Derby were at last starting to do something about reviving former glories. And although he decided to take the plunge, he admits it was something of a calculated risk.

"They were in the Third Division and that's quite a bit below First Division standard," he says.

"The only thing was, I could sense what might be about to happen at the Baseball Ground. Everyone in football knows about Derby County — they were so big a few years ago, they won the League Championship. I had the feeling the new manager Arthur Cox would go a long way to bringing back those good times to the club."

Great gates

Gregory admits it has been an exciting period for the club. And he is optimistic that Derby's future can be just as good.

He says: "When we were going along nicely in the Second, we were averaging about 15,000 gates. That is a whole lot better than a lot of First Division clubs these days.

"The great thing Arthur Cox has done, however, is to bury the memory of Brian Clough at Derby County. Sure, what Cloughie did was terrific during his time here but the club cannot look back to former glories."

At 33, Gregory is clearly running out of time in playing a significant long term role in Derby County's fortunes. He is realistic enough to accept that. But he still believes the club can go on to secure a good future and banish completely memories of the dark days when they slid all the way down to Division Three.

"As a First Division club Derby expect to take £1 million in season ticket sales," says Gregory. "And with that kind of money and support, they will always be able to play a significant role in the transfer market.

"That much was proven by the club's decision to buy Nigel Callaghan from Watford for £140,000 early in 1987. Not many Second Division clubs could do that these days.

"This is and always will be a big club, potentially one of the top 10 in the country.

"Brian Clough put the club on the map but this is now a new era and one which might be almost as successful in the long term. Who knows?"

VIV FOR

VICTORY

Viv Anderson scores England's second goal in a vital European Championship game against Yugoslavia at Wembley in November, 1986. Whether he's defending, or on the attack for England and Arsenal, Viv has proved himself a real winner!

BARCELO BO

Mark Hughes (left) and Gary Lineker.

F.C.B.

Barcelona is not just a football club — it has become the voice and spirit of a people still regarding themselves as fiercely independent from the rest of Spain.

Barcelona is in Catalonia, a region of Spain as different in the minds of its people as, say, the Basque region on the Atlantic side of the country.

When Civil War broke out in Spain in 1936 Barcelona was the headquarters of the International Brigade which opposed General Franco.

But the long, bitter Civil War brought disaster not just to Spain itself but especially Catalonia.

Franco's victory meant repression for the Catalan people. They were banned from using their own language in official residences, public buildings and such places. The Catalan idea was suppressed.

But at one place the language could be used — Barcelona Football Club. And so the club became the focal point of opposition to Franco who was based in Madrid.

Matches between Barcelona and the Madrid clubs, Real and Atletico, became much more than football games — in the eyes of the Catalan people in Barcelona, they provided the chance to prove their superiority over the representatives of Madrid.

As Leo Bennhakker, coach of Real Madrid says: "Barcelona against Real Madrid is much more than a football match. It is about politics and it is about religion."

Nothing, says Barcelona's England striker Gary Lineker, can compare with a match between the two leading clubs in Spain.

"Certainly, a game like Everton against Liverpool in the English League would not be in the least bit comparable."

Barcelona enjoy phenomenal support. They have 110,000 season ticket holders generating a staggering income worth millions of pounds every year.

The income makes the club probably the most wealthy in all of Europe for the swank Nou Camp stadium holds 120,000 people and is always full for the big games. Average gates for ordinary League matches are around 90,000.

England star Lineker cost the club £2.8 million from Everton; Welshman Mark Hughes was a £2 million signing from Manchester United. But as well as signing those two overseas stars around the same time, manager Terry Venables also bought goalkeeper Zubizeretta from Bilbao and midfield international Roberto, from Valencia.

These two cost more than £1 million to go with the near £5 million outlay on Hughes and Lineker — all for the same season.

Lineker earns around £400,000 a season with bonuses of £500 a game.

Nothing can compare with Real Madrid (all white) v. Barcelona clashes.

NA NANZA!

Venables IN – Maradona OUT

Terry Venables (right) with Allan Harris.

Terry Venables has enjoyed remarkable success as coach to Barcelona. His arrival as the successor to Argentine manager Cesar Luis Menotti was greeted with scorn and a torrent of disapproval by the critical supporters of the club used to seeing only the most famous arrive to take charge.

National managers like Menotti, the Dutchman Rinus Michels (the last man to steer Barcelona to the Spanish Championship title before Venables managed it in his first season), the West German Hennese Weisweiller and another German, Udo Lattek who had taken Bayern Munich to the European Cup Final, have all been handed one of the toughest jobs in sport.

Michels once said ''Managing this football club is like managing no other on earth. Who can understand the enormous pressures of guiding a club which an entire nation (Catalonia) wants to see successful. It is an incredible task.''

Into the whirlpool of supreme tension stepped Venables and his faithful No. 2 Allan Harris. Yet the criticism was intense. 'Who is this unknown — how can mighty Barcelona take on a man no one has ever heard of' said some supporters.

Venables had gone to Barcelona

continued overleaf

BARCELONA BONANZA!

continued

because Menotti had advised the club the Englishman was the man to take on. Although only with the moderate West London club Q.P.R., Venables had proved his pedigree to those in the know in world football.

What Venables and Harris have done during their stay at the club has been remarkable.

In their first season in charge, they sold off the world's greatest footballer, Diego Maradona the Argentina star, to Italian giants Napoli for a £6.2 million fee.

That roused great anger in Barcelona especially as the only overseas replacement bought was a little known Scot, Steve Archibald who cost £800,000 from Tottenham Hotspur.

But the move turned out to be a master stroke. Without Maradona, Venables built a real team and it was good enough to win the Spanish Championship title for the first time since 1974, by a huge margin of ten points

In the second season of the English pair's reign, Barcelona reached the European Cup Final although they lost it, disastrously, on penalties to the Rumanian club Steaua Bucharest.

And in their third season, Barcelona went to the top of the Spanish League table right at the start of the campaign and stayed there for most of the winter.

Great achievements which turned the people who had sneered at the arrival of the Englishmen into loyal fans!

Cruyff magic

Barcelona's vast financial resources have meant they have been able to buy some of the greatest stars the world game has ever known.

Some of Spain's greatest footballers have played for the club. But it is the world stars who have really captured the imagination over the past 15 years.

Johan Cruyff, the brilliant Dutchman, had just steered the Netherlands into the World Cup Final of 1974 when he agreed to join Barcelona, from Ajax Amsterdam, the club he had helped to three European Cup titles.

Cruyff was recruited by his national manager, Rinus Michels. And between them they lifted Barcelona in extraordinary style.

When Cruyff first got to Barcelona, it was mid-September and after the first few matches he played, the club was bottom of the table and heading for disaster.

But suddenly, Cruyff turned on

the magic, together with his fellow Dutchman *Johan Neeskens.* The pair played so well that Barcelona went straight up the table into first place and stayed there for the rest of the season, winning the title for the first time in 14 years.

But other stars arrived, in a flood of money. The brilliant Dane, *Allan Simonsen,* who was to become Footballer of the Year in Europe, helped Barcelona to the European Cup Winners' Cup title at the end of the 1970's.

Diego Maradona went to Barcelona from Argentina but did not make the impact imagined. He was cruelly injured by some cynical Spanish defenders and moved on to Napoli when Venables took over.

Before that, *Bernd Schuster,* the brilliant but temperamental West German international star, was also signed. Further back, *Hugo Sotil* the Peruvian international was there and, more recently, the Scottish international *Steve Archibald,* English hot shot *Gary Lineker* and Welsh strongman striker *Mark Hughes,* who have failed to hit it off together. But the club could remedy that by again spending big in the transfer market.

Left: Deigo Maradona was sensationally sold to Napoli.
Below: The great Johan Cruyff helped save the club from disaster.

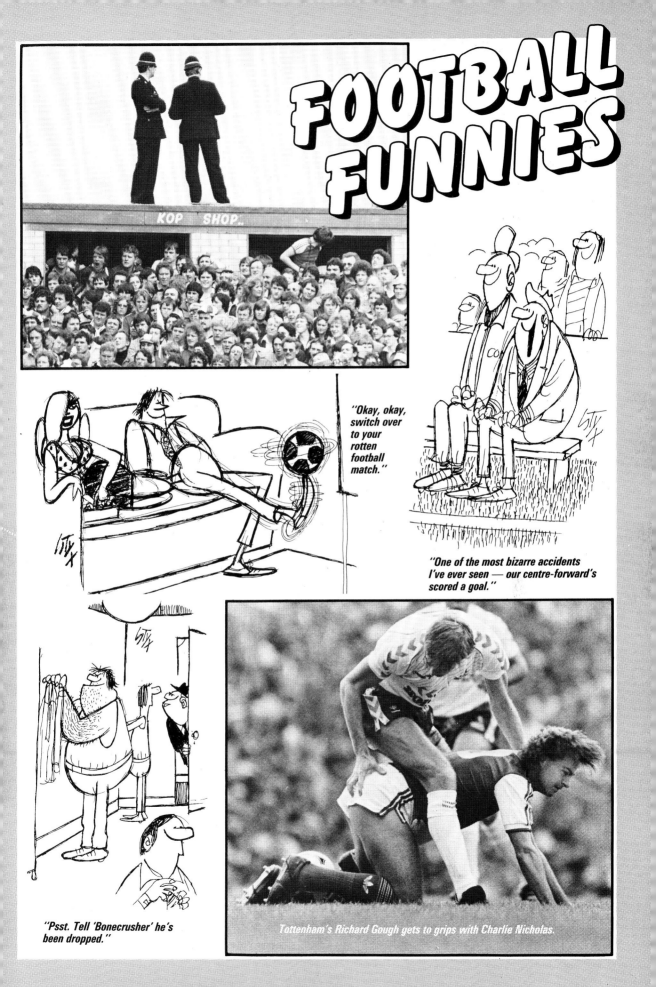

FOOTBALL FUNNIES

KOP SHOP..

"Okay, okay, switch over to your rotten football match."

"One of the most bizarre accidents I've ever seen — our centre-forward's scored a goal."

"Psst. Tell 'Bonecrusher' he's been dropped."

Tottenham's Richard Gough gets to grips with Charlie Nicholas.

Youngsters destined for the top in Scotland . . .

We all know of the likes of Kenny Dalglish, Denis Law, Jimmy Johnstone, Jim Baxter, Graeme Souness and Dave Mackay, a veritable parade of Scottish power and poise.

But who are the new players about to explode on the Scottish scene over the coming months? SHOOT turns the spotlight on eight who could be great in '88!

MARK SMITH, the lightning-swift Celtic winger, is the "golden oldie" of our selection of youngsters to watch — and he's just turned 23!

Smith, who joined the Parkhead side from Queen's Park in the summer of '86, is so determined to make it big that he was put on a diet of pasta last season!

"The Celtic doctor decided I needed building-up and I had to agree with him," admits Smith. "After all, I don't exactly look like Rambo!

"When I first tried to break

Super Sub David McFarland (back row first left) helped Rangers beat Celtic in the 1986 Skol Cup Final at Hampden.

Super

Celtic veteran Danny McGrain has a problem with Aberdeen's exciting young striker Paul Knight.

through in football I was annoyed at continually being told I was too skinny. A couple of clubs turned me away before I signed amateur forms with Queen's Park.

"As luck would have it, we were drawn against Celtic in the Scottish Cup that season and, although we lost 2–1 at Parkhead, I must have made a fairly good impression on manager Davie Hay.

"He signed me shortly afterwards and I've enjoyed myself thoroughly ever since. Now I'm looking forward to '88 — that will be a vital year for me."

DAVID MacFARLANE, 20, created such an immediate good impression with manager Graeme Souness last season that the Ibrox supremo gave him a substitute's role in the Skol Cup Final against Celtic.

MacFarlane, a hard-working midfielder, came on during a frantic second-half and helped Souness to his first trophy success as Rangers' boss, beating

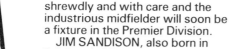

shrewdly and with care and the industrious midfielder will soon be a fixture in the Premier Division.

JIM SANDISON, also born in Edinburgh 22 years ago, has been known to creat a little bit of confusion in the Hearts rearguard when he has made first team appearances.

''People keep confusing me for my Tynecastle team-mate Neil Berry,'' says Sandison. ''I suppose we are a bit similar with curly blond hair and the same build.

''Just so long as I play with the same sort of determination and professionalism you won't hear me complaining.''

Across Edinburgh at Easter Road, 19-year-old JOHN COLLINS is beginning to make his presence felt in the Hibs midfield.

8 for '88

Collins is a gifted midfielder who likes to make the ball do the work. He sprays passes around with the grace of a seasoned campaigner and manager Alex Miller says: ''When you look at a teenager such as John in action you realise the game in Scotland is in a very healthy state.''

Another midfielder who could one day challenge Collins, McLeod and MacFarlane for a place in the

Dundee's Robert Shannon looks forward to a bright future.

the old enemy 2–1.

PAUL WRIGHT became a first team regular at Aberdeen as soon as Ian Porterfield took over as manager last season when Alex Ferguson left for Manchester United.

''He struck me as a player who would build up his confidence with a string of games — and that's what happened,'' says Porterfield.

Wright, only 20, was born in East Kilbride on the outskirts of Glasgow, but Celtic and Rangers both missed out on this soccer jewel.

Dundee United have brought up some fresh and exciting talent over the recent years in the shape of Andy Gray, Richard Gough, Ray Stewart, Paul Sturrock, Maurice Malpas and David Narey.

GORDON McLEOD, born in Edinburgh 20 years ago, is another babe tipped to rocket into the headlines.

Tannadice manager Jim McLean has shaped the youngster's career

Jim Sandison created some confusion in the Hearts back-four.

full Scottish international team is St. Mirren's 20-year-old IAN FERGUSON.

The Saints paid £80,000 for his exceptional talents last season after the Glasgow-born ball-player had spent only one year as a senior with Clyde.

''He's the sort of player who will run all day for you,'' says Saints' boss Alex Smith. ''Ian always gives his all and I was delighted to inherit such a player when I left Stirling Albion to take over at Love Street last year.''

ROBERT SHANNON, of Dundee, is last but obviously not least in our list of kids with stars in their eyes . . . a 22-year-old who has already proved he can do a man's job in soccer.

He's been a first team regular for Dundee for the past two seasons and is a buccaneering full-back who thrills crowds and terrifies 'keepers with his explosive shooting.

Keep your eyes on these eight lads . . . they're destined to be great in '88!

YOU ARE THE REF

1 A goalkeeper, whose team is losing heavily, leaves his goal unattended to join in his side's attack. Do you (a) take no action or (b) instruct him to return to his goal?

2 You have stopped play, but the attacking team do not hear your whistle and score. What action do you take?

3 At a free-kick near goal an attacker stations himself in front of the ball. Opponents forming a "wall" protest. Do you (a) take no action or (b) caution him?

4 A corner-kick is taken quickly after the ball is placed outside the corner quadrant. Do you (a) take no action or (b) order the kick to be retaken?

5

A: A defender obstructs an opponent and pushes him at the last moment. You award a free-kick.

B: Before defending players have time to move ten yards from the ball an opponent places the ball and kicks it to a team-mate who shoots. You do not stop play.

C: The ball is caught by the 'keeper. He rolls it to a team-mate who touches it before it goes out of the box. You award an indirect free-kick. (Where is the problem?)

ANSWERS

1. Take no action (a). There is no restriction on his movement.
2. The goal is not valid. Restart by dropping the ball where it was when you stopped play. 3. Take no action (a). The attacker is not committing an offence. 4. The kick must be retaken (b) with the ball correctly placed inside the quadrant. 5. The problem is in C. When the ball is in play it is not necessary to wait for it to clear the penalty-area before touching it. In A a direct free-kick is correctly awarded because pushing an opponent is a more serious offence than obstruction, for which an indirect free-kick is the award. In B the advantage has been correctly allowed for the benefit of the attacking team who wish to take the free-kick as quickly as possible.

PETER
BEARDSLEY
ENGLAND

Football's most face-to-face interview

Q: Yes.
A: Just a few little things I suppose; socks, boxer shorts, a tie, a tie pin, some chocolate, a Christmas card, a little key ring and a Mercedes sports car.
Q: Did you have it tough as a kid . . . I hear you could scarcely afford football boots?
A: Football boots! Luxury! Ah' played wi' 'obnailed boots. Couldn't afford a ball. We used ta nick a lump 'o coal to play wi' mates

Q: Hello Pat, it's good to meet you. How are you doing?
A: Oh, it's you Pat. Please excuse me, I didn't recognise you in mens clothing. What I mean is I usually see you stripped . . . that is, with your football kit on.
Q: Are you feeling all right?
A: It's the shrapnel you see. Picked it up in 'Nam.
Q: Were you in Vietnam?
A: No, Cheltenham. (Ta, Ted)
Q: Tell me Pat, why did I decide to interview you?
A: Frankly, I'm doing it for the money.
Q: Are you sure it's not that previous interviewers insist on portraying you as some sort of quaint curio, no more than a likeable misfit, with a penchant for pseudo-intellectualising on the role of the competitive sportsman in today's society.
A: Nope, it was for the money — really.
Q: Tell me Pat, who is my . . . your favourite player?
A: I've got a few. Laudrup and Maradona, and Tony McAndrew, an old Chelsea team-mate of mine, is one of the best pros I've ever had the pleasure of being kicked by in training.
Q: What then, do you consider to be the main qualities needed in a good pro?

A: I'd expect him to be reliable, someone I could have complete confidence in. I would expect strength as well as the ability to give the gentle touch; durability as well as a clean tackler. Not many players possess all these qualities, but there are quite a few toilet rolls that fit the bill quite nicely.
Q: What is the most banal question you've ever been asked during an interview?
A: Quite
Q: OK, apart from this question what was the most banal?
A: A "top" sports journalist once asked: "Now you have lost your first team place, are you going to try to get it back?"
Q: Which headline would you most like to see in 1988?
A: "John Inman gets England call." The former Grace Brothers impressario quipped "I'm tickled . . . or at least I hope to be."
Q: What don't you like about the game just now?
A: Unprofessionalism, vandalism, sectarianism, tribalism, two sweepers as a defence mechanism, unconstructive criticism, galloping capitalism and cheque book journalism.
Q: What do you want for Christmas?
A: Apart from a Dukla Prague away kit?

Denmark's Michael Laudrup

NEVIN

mazing ace ...

in t' street. Then mam would come out an' bash us for using t' precious coal. We'd end up playing wi 'alf a brick — an' even then we had ta play in t' street bare footed for fear of scuffin' thee boots.

Q: Tell me Pat why are you . . . er hum . . . "less than renowned" for your heading ability?

A: Ah'd like t'see thee learn to head 'alf a brick.

Q: Oh why don't you belt up, you bore.

A: Sorry Brian . . . er . . . Pat.

Q: Do you still enjoy playing football?

A: I always used to say that when I stopped enjoying it I'd pack it in and I hope this still holds true. Luckily I'm one of those players who constantly realises how good a job he's got. Not that many people get well paid for doing their hobby. A footballer's lot isn't bad, but it isn't easy. I like to get pushed towards physical and emotional limits. This is when you discover your own true qualities and strengths.

Q: What will you do when you finish playing?

A: Have a bath, probably. Then perhaps I'll write a book on some of my experiences within football. I've already started it, as a matter of fact.

Q: What is your profession as stated on your passport and what will it be in 10 years time?

A: Just now it is student. In 10 years who knows — entrepreneur? Philanthropist? Journalist? Kept man? I'll think about it when the time comes.

Q: Thanks for the time, Pat. Did you enjoy it?

A: Yes, it was wonderful.

Q: I know. It was wonderful for me too, cheeky.

FOUR TOP STRIKERS REVEAL...
THE GOAL THAT CHANGED

John Deehan scored twice for Aston Villa in their 2–2 draw at QPR in a 1977 League Cup-tie.

John Deehan — Ipswich Town
for Aston Villa v QPR Semi-Final 1976–77 League Cup.

It's the first of the two goals I scored as an Aston Villa player to earn us a 2–2 draw with QPR in the Semi-Final second-leg of the 1976–77 League Cup competition. My performance convinced the boss I was worth a place in the team and wouldn't get swept away, overwhelmed, if we reached Wembley. We did just that after a 3–1 decider at Highbury — Brian Little getting a hat-trick. I kept my place in a real 'Marathon' of a Final, going to two replays, and became the proud possessor of a winner's medal.

Paul Sturrock — Dundee United
for Scotland v Portugal World Cup qualifier, November 1981.

I was competing with a lot of strikers for a place in the Scotland World Cup squad going to Spain in 1982 — and this golden goal gave me my passport. We were playing Portugal in Lisbon. A long through ball dropped over my head. The 'keeper was favourite to get it, but he hesitated for a split-second. I saw my chance and volleyed the ball into the net — and myself into the squad. Although I didn't get a game in Spain, I can at least boast that I was there — courtesy of a goal I'll certainly never forget!

Ian Rush — Juventus

for Liverpool v Everton 1986 FA Cup Final.

The first goal in the Cup Final of 1986 must rank as the most important of my life.

We were losing 1–0 to a Gary Lineker goal at the time and when I equalised it seemed to give the team new sense and belief in ourselves.

The lads all knew that we'd never lost

MY LIFE

Ian Rush takes the ball around Everton 'keeper Bobby Mimms to grab Liverpool's equaliser in the 1986 F.A. Cup Final.

in a game that I'd scored in, and the goal seemed to be the turning point in the match.

It wasn't the most spectacular goal I'll score by any means. Jan Molby put a good ball through and I latched on to it before taking it round Bobby Mimms and sidefooting into the empty net. The goal set us on the way to the Double, and not many teams do that. It was also my first FA Cup Final and the fact the match was against Everton made it all the more memorable.

Kerry Dixon — Chelsea

for Chelsea v Grimsby last Saturday of the 1983–84 season.

I have scored more than 100 goals since bursting onto the League scene with Reading in 1980, but I don't hesitate when asked to name the most important strike of my life so far.

The goal that clinched the Second Division title for Chelsea in 1984 stands out.

It was a header from a Pat Nevin cross scored at Grimsby on the final day of the season.

The club had never won the Second Division title before so it was a proud day for myself and for the club. And what made the goal even more special was that it took my League total for the season to 28 — one ahead of Kevin Keegan's total for Newcastle — meaning I won the SHOOT/Adidas Golden Shoe award.

Kerry Dixon celebrates his Second Division Championship clincher at Grimsby.

While Terry Butcher's career has rocketed since leaving Ipswich for Rangers, his former Portman Road partner Russell Osman has slipped quietly out of the limelight.

But while Butcher has gone on to win more than 50 caps for his country, Osman is in the international wilderness.

A subsequent move to Leicester City has done little to reinforce Osman's claims for a recall, yet the powerful centre-half remains one of the game's most consistent defenders.

Paul's Anfield aim...

Paul Walsh has never had it easy in his two and a half years at Liverpool.

Unable to oust Ian Rush and Kenny Dalglish when he arrived from Luton in a £750,000 deal, injury further hampered his progress when he did eventually break into the first team at Anfield.

But Rush's summer transfer to Juventus and Dalglish's retirement have finally pushed Walsh centre stage . . . and he's determined to make the most of his opportunity.

''Ian and Kenny were the two greatest strikers in the British game when I arrived,'' he recalls. ''I learned so much just watching them in action together and I hope to put that knowledge to good use with John Aldridge.

''Because it took me quite a while to string together a decent run of first team performances, there has been a lot of speculation that my future lies elsewhere.

''But my aim has always been to prove myself with the biggest and best club in the game and to win further England caps. That has not changed.''

WHO has got the hardest shot in Scottish football?

Scottish international 'keeper Billy Thomson, who has faced a barrage of efforts over the past decade with Partick Thistle, St. Mirren and now Dundee United, has no doubts.

''It's got to be my Tannadice team-mate John Clark,'' says Thomson. ''He'll have a pop from anywhere and when he gets behind his effort you really feel it.

''Thank goodness I only have to face him in training, although that is difficult enough, believe me.

''I wonder If I could pick up danger money for training with John!''

What does one of Scotland's most overworked goalkeepers, Dave McKellar, of Hamilton Accies, think?

''I agree 100 per cent,'' says the former Carlisle, Hibs and Newcastle 'keeper. ''Clark's mighty drives simply boom down at you with awesome pace.

''He's a big lad and he's not afraid to have a go. Anywhere in your own half is a danger area when he's got the ball at his feet.

''He not only hits the ball powerfully, but with a fair degree of accuracy, too. That doesn't make a goalkeeper's job any easier.

''Normally when you face a player who simply blasts the ball you know he is not going to try to

MASTER BLASTER CLARK

place it.

''However, Clark has the ability to hit the ball with devastating power without having to sacrifice any accuracy. He's quite a fearsome customer when he's in the mood.''

Why then doesn't John Clark figure more prominently in the Premier Division goalscorer's chart?

He answers: ''I started off as a striker, but I wasn't getting into the right positions. I was being crowded out and manager Jim McLean thought it would be a good idea to give me a new role.''

The astute McLean, who plotted a transformation in Paul Hegarty's career when he moved him from an old-fashioned centre-forward to a calculating centre-back where he went on to represent his country, worked the same switch with Clark.

Master Blaster Clark takes most of Dundee United's direct free-kicks along with Eamonn Bannon. But while Bannon will work the cunning lob to catch the 'keeper out, the defensive wall look on petrified as Clark lets loose with another deadly venomous effort.

MARTIN HAYES

East

The fictional borough of Walford produced a massive hit for the BBC when they launched EastEnders in 1985.

Walthamstow, situated in London's real-life East End, has provided another one for Arsenal in the shape of Martin Hayes.

Hayes, born in East London 21 years ago, is an important fixture in an Arsenal side that has really come of age under manager George Graham.

Dubbed 'Boring Arsenal' for more years than the Highbury fans would care to remember, Graham's Gunners have long since made a mockery of that tag. And while classy defender Tony Adams and exciting midfielder David Rocastle have been the names on many people's lips, Hayes has emerged as the most unlikeliest Arsenal star of the lot.

Unlikely, because he was almost shipped off to lowly Huddersfield last season for the sort of transfer fee that wouldn't buy his little finger these days.

Valuable

Now, with his penalty-spot prowess and his attacking sorties from the left side of midfield, Hayes is as valuable to Arsenal as Michelle is to Lofty (an Arsenal supporter, by the way!)

Hayes, with his roots firmly in London, decided against a move and the rest, as they say, is history.

"I must admit I was a little upset when I heard Arsenal had accepted a £25,000 offer for me," remembers Hayes.

"Arsenal was the club where I learned my trade. I played in the schoolboy, youth and reserve sides, and I desperately wanted to continue my education at Highbury.

"I made 14 appearances in the first team before George Graham arrived at the club as boss, and I hoped he would give me a chance to make an impression."

He almost found out to his cost things don't always work out like that.

Hayes, who still admits he feels his best position is on the right side of midfield, could only look on as young Rocastle started to make that position his own.

"It suddenly dawned on me that my time was up at Arsenal," Hayes recalls.

But an injury to Graham Rix gave Hayes a lifeline that he has been grateful for ever since.

Suddenly a place was created, albeit on the substitutes bench, for a Milk Cup-tie at Huddersfield and . . . you've guessed it, Hayes came on and scored.

"It's something you dream about," he says.

Indeed, EastEnders producer Julia Smith — who always insists on realistic storylines — wouldn't have dared use such a plot.

And just to add to the fairytale Hayes kept his place, impressing all who watched, and finished last season as the club's top goalscorer.

Boss Graham admits: "Young Martin has proved me wrong and I am delighted for him.

"He's a good strong runner who always wants the ball, and he has shown what a natural finisher he is."

Graham can think of at least one other reason why he is so glad to have been proven wrong in his early assessment of Hayes.

He points out: "Home grown players like Martin always seem to show more loyalty towards a club.

"If you can nurture them along and treat them right they can become far more attached.

"They're not normally as mercenary in their attitude as the ones you sign from elsewhere, who often want to move on to pastures new after two or three years."

Hammers fan

Certainly team work and a loyalty to the club (although, whisper it softly, Hayes used to watch West Ham as a schoolboy!) seem to be the secret to Arsenal's recent success.

Scottish striker Andy Gray points out: "There is something about the spirit in this Arsenal side that reminds me of the Everton team I was involved in that won the League title in 1985.

"They pull together effectively as a unit. When an opponent has the ball they defend in numbers and when they have the ball they attack together, too.

"Martin seems to be typical of this philosophy. Whenever I've seen him play he works extremely hard." Hayes himself says: "Youngsters like myself are keen.

"We want to make an impression in the game and we'll gladly chase lost causes. Perhaps that is something that more experienced

pros don't do as often." And, when it is considered, the same could apply on the Albert Square set at Elstree. A bunch of relatively unknown actors thrown together, to produce a soap opera to rival the long time favourite from the North, Coronation Street.

Could Liverpool, Everton and Manchester United be about to suffer similar treatment?

We can think of one East Ender who certainly hopes so.

ender star

While Tony Adams (left) grabbed the headlines, Martin Hayes quietly established himself at Arsenal.

FOOTBALL

The Football League

Notts County became the first League club to be formed in 1862.

The first League season was in 1888–89 with Preston winning the Championship without losing a game. They also won the FA Cup to complete the first double.

Burnley's Walter Tait scored the first hat-trick in the League in his club's 4–3 victory over Bolton on September 15th, 1888.

How appropriate that Tottenham, who introduced the trend of importing overseas stars when they bought Argentinans Osvaldo Ardiles and Ricky Villa in 1978, should have paraded the first foreign player. A German called Max Seeburg made his debut for the club in the 1908–09 season.

Bolton's 1–0 victory against Blackpool in 1960 was the first game shown live on TV. The match was so poor that plans to show more live matches was shelved.

Keith Peacock became the first substitute to be used when he came on for Charlton against Bolton on August 21st, 1965.

Scottish League

Dumbarton and Rangers shared the first Scottish Championship after finishing level on points and then drawing 2–2 in a play-off.

James Gordon of Rangers was a rather versatile player to say the least. Between 1910 and 1930 he played in every position for the Ibrox club. Another first was the performances of Greenock Morton in 1912–13. Every member of their squad scored a League goal.

Jimmy McGrory became the first player to average a goal a game in a complete career in British football. He scored 410 goals in 408 matches.

Dundee United's Paul Sturrock (right) was the first player to score five goals in a Scottish Premier League match against Morton in November 1984.

Cup Matches

Wanderers beat Royal Engineers with a goal by Matthew Betts to win the first FA Cup Final in 1872 at the Kennington Oval.

Queens Park, the first Scottish League club founded in 1867, won the opening Scottish Cup Final when they beat Clydedale in 1874. William McKinnon scored their first goal in the 2–0 victory.

Queens Park, the best side in the world at the time, were the first club to appear in the Scottish and FA Cup in the same season. In 1884 they were awarded the trophy North of the border because their opponents Vale of Lethen failed to turn up. But a unique double was spoilt by Blackburn Rovers who beat them 2–1 in the English Final.

Stan Mortensen became the first player to score a hat-trick in an FA Cup Final for Blackpool in their 4–3 victory over Bolton.

Stan Mortensen on his way to a hat-trick for Blackpool in the famous 1953 F.A. Cup Final.

41 matches passed before an FA Cup Final was drawn and had to go to a replay. Chelsea and Leeds finished 2–2 in the 1970 Final with The Blues winning the replay 2–1 at Old Trafford.

Kevin Moran became the first player to be sent-off in an FA Cup Final when playing for Manchester United against Everton in 1985. 119 Finals had passed before Moran received his marching orders.

In Europe

The first British club to participate in the European Cup were Hibernian in 1955–56. They lost to runners-up Stade de Reims in the Semi-Final.

Celtic were the first British winners of the European Cup when they beat Inter Milan in 1969. A year later Manchester United became the first English club to achieve that success when they beat Benfica 4–1 at Wembley.

The first European Final to be contested by two English clubs was in 1971–72 when Spurs beat Wolves 3–2 on aggregate to win the UEFA Cup.

John Wark was on the spot when he became the first player to score three penalties in a European competition. Wark added a fourth goal as Ipswich beat Aris Salonika in the UEFA Cup in 1980–81 season.

FIRSTS

Being first can bring you fame, fortune and land you in the record books.

We have taken a selection of achievements, some spectacular, some surprising, some amusing but all are history-making firsts.

Above: Laurie Cunningham, a £1 million free transfer. Left: Italy's Cavrini misses from the penalty-spot during the 1982 World Cup Final against West Germany.

Internationals

Scotland and England drew 0–0 in the first official international match in 1872.

France had a slight advantage in the first-half of their 3–1 win at home to Northern Ireland in 1952 — they had 12 players on the pitch. Their player Bonifaci was substituted but inadvertently returned to the play after receiving treatment for an injury. The error was only spotted at the interval in what was the first incident of its kind.

England's Billy Wright was the first player to win 100 caps.

Scotland became the first country to have their names printed on their shirts when they drew with Peru in 1979.

World Cup

Uruguay became the first winners of the trophy when they beat Argentina 4–2 in 1930.

Luisito Monti became the first player to play in two Finals for different countries when, after appearing for Argentina in the 1930 Final, he played for Italy in their 1934 win over Czechoslovakia.

Mexican goalkeeper Antonia Carbajal appeared in five World Cup Finals series between 1959 and 1966. The first and so far only player to do so.

Antonio Cabrini became the first player to miss a penalty in a World Cup Final when he shot wide in Italy's 3–1 win over West Germany in 1982.

Odd Facts

In 1965, Stanley Matthews became the first player knighted.

Trevor Francis' move from Birmingham to Nottingham Forest in 1979 was the first £1 million transfer deal.

Laurie Cunningham's form nosedived when he joined Real Madrid in 1979. Five years later he became the first £1 million player to be given a free transfer.

Colin Harris making his debut for Dundee scored his first goal with his first touch in the first minute of a League match v. Rangers in 1984.

Can't catch Cottee

First Division defenders have been trying in vain for five years, and now several Italian clubs have found out too . . . you just can't catch West Ham's Tony Cottee.

Still only 22, Cottee has already scored well over 100 League and Cup goals for The Hammers, since getting on the scoresheet on his Division One debut against London rivals Tottenham on New Year's Day 1983.

And those figures have not surprisingly been noted in Italy, where managers and scouts have long since been keen to make the talented West Ham striker England's latest export.

Last season, for example, Atalanta saw the pocket sized goal poacher as the ideal replacement for Trevor Francis.

And Fiorentina and Inter-Milan were also reported to be ready to splash out over £1m for his talents.

But Cottee says: "Although it is flattering to think that one or two Italian clubs might be interested in me I think it is too early for me to be considering anything like a move abroad.

"In two years time I might feel differently, but at the moment I am still going through the learning process and there is no better place to do that than at West Ham."

Cottee, though, will consider following the likes of Gary Lineker and Ian Rush abroad when he considers the time is right.

"And only then," he adds, "if a really big club came in for me with a very, very special offer. I wouldn't move abroad simply for the sake of it."

That's good news for West Ham manager John Lyall and the Upton Park supporters . . . but bad for the rest of the First Division.

The dynamic little England striker hasn't completely ruled out a move to the Continent.

Cottee has built up a fearsome reputation. He is rather like Argentina's Diego Maradona in as much as he is extremely powerful for such a little fella. He's just 5ft 8ins, but tips the scales at around 11st 7lbs.

And his tremendous acceleration and agility in tight situations makes it difficult for many big defenders to keep up with their opponent.

Arsenal's David O'Leary jokes: "As far as I'm concerned the sooner Tony goes off to Italy the better."

He adds: "Tony is a very good young player who has worked hard on all aspects of his game. Certainly I have noticed an improvement in him as a player over the past couple of years.

"He loves nothing more than to score goals and he is extremely dangerous in an around the penalty box."

O'Leary, who has been fending off First Division strikers with aplomb for more than 10 years now, rates the Cottee-Frank McAvennie partnership at Upton Park favourably.

He says: "I am sure Tony would give thanks to Frank for help in his development.

"They have become one of the League's most feared partnerships and we at Arsenal know we're in for a tough time if those two are facing us.

"Tony and Frank have the ability to be able to take up good positions to receive the ball, and make great runs behind defenders."

Best ever

McAvennie's arrival at Upton Park — from St. Mirren for £350,000 in 1985 — did much to take the spotlight away from Cottee's progress.

The Scottish striker netted 26 League goals in his first season South of the border to Cottee's 20 as West Ham recorded their best ever season in the First Division.

But Cottee — born in West Ham and a product of the club's highly respected youth system — took the lead from his partner last season, and also found time to break his way into the senior England squad for the first time after winning Youth and Under-21 caps.

His introduction to international football was low-key, making his first two appearances against Sweden (friendly) and Northern-Ireland as a substitute.

But there can be no doubt that Cottee is one for the future. He is younger than Lineker, Peter Beardsley, Mark Hateley and Clive Allen, for example.

"I'm certainly not short of fire power," says England manager Bobby Robson.

That can only be good news for England as Robson prepares for the European Championship Finals and ultimately the 1990 World Cup Finals, when the Italians might well just catch their first glimpses of goalscorer Cottee.

BRYAN ROBSON

What it's like to join th

'We are flying at 35,000 feet over the Bay of Biscay. The weather is fine. Our scheduled time of arrival at Luton is 2.0 a.m.'

The England team are heading home from Spain after another successful excursion.

The players are tired but they can still hear 'Rule Britannia' ringing in their ears, our fans' response to our 4-2 thrashing of Spain in the mighty Bernabeu Stadium.

In the air, the champagne corks are popping. Soft drinks on the journey out have given way to the bubbly. It's Bobby Robson's birthday . . . and we are celebrating.

As England captain it is my pleasant duty to make a presentation. I am clutching a valuable piece of porcelain we have bought in Madrid.

The Boss gets the shock of his life when I interrupt a conversation he is having with Manchester United manager Alex Ferguson.

'Boss, Happy Birthday from all the team' I announce over the cabin intercom before handing Bobby the piece of china.

Half an hour later the 'plane is making a perfect landing in arctic conditions at Luton Airport.

The flight captain was spot on. It is 2.0 a.m. There are no supporters to greet us. Not many Customs men about either. I nose my Jaguar up the M1 in conversation with Alex Ferguson, who has flown to both England games that day to check on the biggest and best in English football.

It is well after 5.0 a.m. when I crawl into bed at my home in the

Fred Street eased Bryan's pain in Mexico.

BUB
. . . AT 35,0

lovely county of Cheshire.

Playing for England is a wonderful experience but there is something even more special about representing your country abroad.

I got the bug at my first World Cup, in Spain in 1982. I was something of a 'rookie' on that trip under Ron Greenwood, yet to make my 20th England appearance.

Let me tell you a little about playing 'away' with England.

The Football Association know as much about making life comfortable for England players abroad as the best travel agent does for holidaymakers taking their annual trip to the Continent.

Our 1986 World Cup hotel in Saltillo, 80km out of Monterrey was so good I could have stayed there for life.

We shared cabins in the grounds of the main building with a mountain range in the distance and the Mexican sun burning our backs all day.

Handling the media can be a problem on tour. Bobby Robson held more Press conferences on our World Cup trip to Mexico than

Ronald Reagan has attended in his full term of office.

I doubt whether there is a happier international set-up in the world than the one I have had the privilege of knowing since the start of the Eighties.

We receive the full support of Football Association officialdom on our trips overseas, headed by Chairman Bert Millichip.

Firm but fair and extremely personable is Mr. Millichip. Nobody wants to protect the image of

Above: Gary Lineker and Bryan help Bobby Robson celebrate his 54th birthday in style. Below: Chris Woods is set to take over from Peter Shilton.

football better than him.

But don't get him talking cricket. He knows as much about the summer game as he does football.

Administration officer on journeys abroad is Alan O'dell, a superb organiser and ambassador, and Glen Kirton handles the Press.

The new England team doctor is Dr John Crane, who looks as fit as the players. He's attached to Arsenal and is a worthy successor to Dr Vernon Edwards, who has done so much for Watford.

Talking of fitness, we mustn't forget the two England physiotherapists, Fred Street and Norman Medhurst. I have had cause to be grateful to their 'miracle cures' more than most with the string of injuries I have suffered in my England career.

They were the two who came to my rescue when my shoulder 'went' again in England's World Cup game against Morocco in Monterrey.

Sitting in the dressing room nursing my injury, I was surprised to see Ray Wilkins join me a few moments after my pitch exit.

''Is it half-time, Ray?'' I asked. ''No'' he snapped. ''I've been sent off.''

Ray was a marvellous servant to England. Eighty-four appearances spread over ten years and three clubs — Chelsea, Manchester

United, AC Milan — testify to his contribution.

But even Ray gives ground when you examine Peter Shilton's England record. He is England's most capped goalkeeper.

What isn't generally known is that Shilts is one of the most successful England captains ever. His record — four wins, four draws in eight games.

Of recent introductions to the England set-up, I can see the youngsters carrying on the traditions fashioned by the Shiltons, Clemences, and Wilkins of this world.

Rangers goalkeeper Chris Woods won't be 30 until 1989. Fiercely determined to become successor to Peter Shilton, no England player trains harder or more enthusiastically than Woodsie.

Steve Hodge made a sensational breakthrough in Mexico on our World Cup trip and can only get better after joining Spurs from Aston Villa.

Then there's little Peter Beardsley, who has that rare talent for turning in a superb England performance when he's not producing fireworks at League level.

Peter won't be 30 till 1991, and nor will Clive Allen, the Spurs goal-machine.

There is no room for sentiment in international football but I have been tremendously impressed by Bobby Robson's loyalty to players.

The Boss stood by me when half the English Press were writing me off as 'finished'.

Bobby Robson, Bert Millichip, Ted Croker, the F.A. Secretary, and Don Howe, understudy to the Boss for so long, have done so much to keep the Good Ship England sailing on course to a golden future.

Bryan Robson.

£2 million McStay

NOT

ASK Davie Hay the best signing he has ever made and there isn't even the merest trace of hesitation as he snaps back his reply: ''Roy Aitken and Paul McStay.''

Both Aitken and McStay, Scottish international regulars, were coming to the end of their contracts with Celtic when Hay took over the managerial reins back in June, 1983.

''I knew immediately if I was going to be a success in this job

I had to make certain the best players remained at Parkhead," says Hay.

"There was no way I was going to allow Aitken and McStay to leave. I offered them both long-term contracts and was delighted when both signed."

McStay's decision to sign a contract of around five years disappointed Liverpool and Manchester United who were hovering around at the time.

FOR SALE!

Arsenal had just signed former Parkhead personality player Charlie Nicholas and the Celtic fans were in no mood to stand by and watch more of their team's top talent drift South.

Inter-Milan were on the scene for McStay and there was talk of a £2 million bid, but Hay laughed it off: "They're wasting their time. We don't want their money. They could double the bid and we would still throw it out. Paul wants to stay here, we want him to stay here and that's the end of it."

Tradition

The polite, soft-spoken McStay, brought up in Larkhall, Lanarkshire, says: "My entire family is steeped in the Celtic tradition and I'm no different.

"My brother Willie was a Celtic player until he joined Huddersfield last March, and my young brother Raymond is still at Parkhead.

"Celtic are a team that gets into your system. Look at my old mate Charlie Nicholas. He's still Celtic daft.

"I know if he ever returned to Scotland the only club he would be interested in playing for is Celtic.

"It was just a shame he left in the first place. I thoroughly enjoyed playing in the same side as cheeky Charlie.

"Of course, we've teamed up in Scotland's colours, too, but it

Above: Willie McStay (left) and brother Paul celebrate Scottish F.A. Cup success over Dundee United in the 1985 Final.
Below: The ever dependable Roy Aitken is also a vital cog in the Celtic machine.

would be nice to think that some day we'll both be wearing the green-and-white again."

McStay's career took off like the proverbial rocket as a raw 17-year-old when the then manager Billy McNeill introduced him to first team action, but there was a slight hiccup a couple of seasons ago.

"Yes, that's true," concedes McStay. "Quite simply, I lost a little bit of confidence and I struggled for a while. Thankfully, with the help of all the lads, I got over it."

Precision

Paul, known as Parkhead's prince of the precision pass, has at least another decade at the very top of his profession and he's being tipped as the man who will go on and pass Kenny Dalglish's 100-plus total of caps for his nation.

"It's a nice thought," says McStay, "but international football is a bonus. It's what happens week in, week out with Celtic that really counts."

Yes, Davie Hay did a good bit of business when he signed his own player!

Wimbledon's sensational rise from non-League obscurity to First Division surprise guys.

BASSETT'S ALLSORTS!

TEN short years transformed Wimbledon Football Club from a non-League outfit to First Division members and F.A. Cup challengers.

The transformation in that short period has been stunning down at Plough Lane in South-West London.

And although former manager Dave Bassett, who was at the helm throughout the crucial years of the club's remarkable progress, says there was no magic secret, Bassett does admit: "Sheer hard work had a great deal to do with it."

assett is the chirpy Cockney who took over as manager in January 1981. Wimbledon had been admitted to the Football League Division Four just four years earlier and achieved promotion at the end of their second season.

But the dream looked like dying as the club went back to the bottom Division in a relegation season. But then came the Bassett whirlwind — and it's still blowing hard.

F.A. Cup favourites Everton, Finalists for three successive seasons and keen to get to Wembley for a fourth successive appearance, discovered the power of the Wimbledon wizards in February, 1986.

They were dumped out of the F.A. Cup at the Fifth Round stage by 3–1, victims of another of Dave Bassett's fierce half-time pep talks which brought so many famous victories.

Bassett, now manager at Watford, recalls: "When you get results like that, it is tempting to look back. But that isn't my way — I prefer to look ahead and hope the club has a bright future even though it may have to be on a new ground away from Plough Lane.

"But I must admit I would never have believed in 1981 what was about to happen. If someone had said all this was around the corner, I'd have laughed. I certainly would not have put any money on Dons being in the First Division at this time."

But if there has been one secret of Bassett's success with Wimbledon it was his ability to bring players of above average ability to the club.

"I always knew Dave Beasant was a better goalkeeper than Fourth Division standard. And I always felt John Fashanu would score goals in Division One."

News of a merger with Crystal Palace because of financial problems and the need to move from Plough Lane made headlines last season.

"Whatever lies ahead I still believe they have a great future," says Dave.

And the ambition of proving the critics wrong is still a considerable motivating factor in Dave Bassett's life. "People say I won't keep it up at Watford. To me that is just another challenge."

Fash' wombling free.

The Dons giant-killing days against mighty Leeds in '75

UP THE DONS!

WIMBLEDON'S rise to the heights of English football has been one of the great success stories of recent times. Their example is an inspiration to all other non-League clubs now offered a chance to progress swiftly through the Football League by the new ruling which provides for automatic promotion/relegation for the winners of the Vauxhall Conference GM League and the bottom club in the Fourth Division.

Several clubs view the new plan with suspicion. But Wimbledon are in favour, especially considering their own rapid rise through the ranks.

Wimbledon's record of triumphs in the Football League is shown in the detailed fact file below . . .

Year formed: 1889
Turned Professional: 1964
Elected to Football League: 1977
League History . . . . . DIVISION 4: Season 1977/78, 1978/79. Won promotion to Division 3 in 1979 by finishing third on goal difference.
DIVISION 3: Season 1979/80. Finished bottom of table.
DIVISION 4: Season 1980/81. Finished fourth to win a promotion place.
DIVISION 3: Season 1981/82. Relegated again to Division 4.
DIVISION 4: Season 1982/83. Champions of the Fourth Division.
DIVISION 3: Season 1983/84. Promoted to Second Division after finishing runners-up to Oxford United.
DIVISION 2: Seasons 1984/85 and 1985/86. Promoted to First Division in May 1986 after finishing third behind Norwich City and Charlton.
DIVISION 1: Seasons 1986/87 and 1987/88.
Made further history in 1986/87 season by reaching Quarter-Finals of the F.A. Cup for the first time in the club's history. Previous best season had been in 1984/85 when they lost in the Fifth Round.

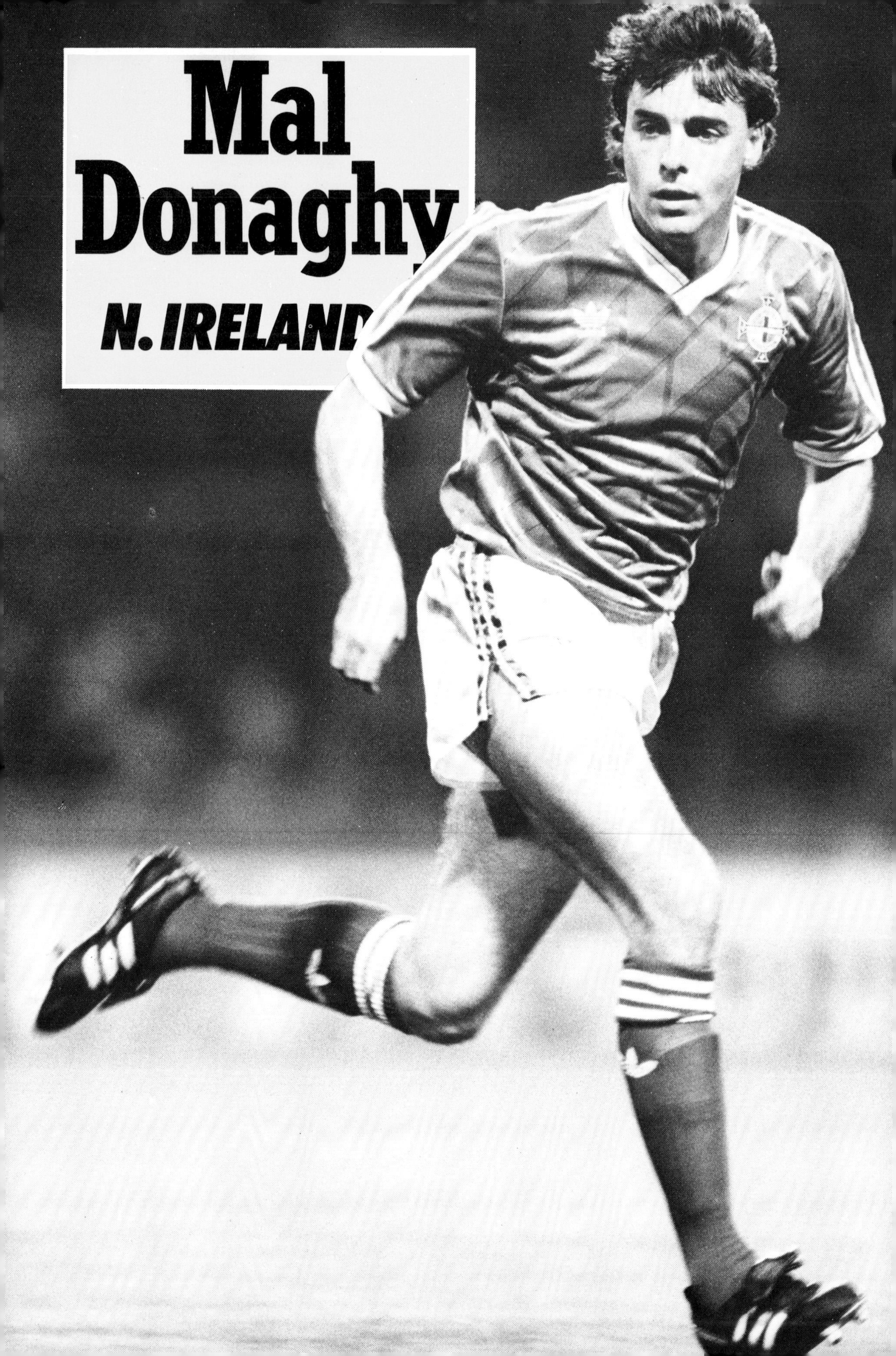
Mal
Donaghy
N. IRELAND

You've got to be a great goalkeeper to still be holding down the number one spot at the ripe age of 36 – and Hibs' Alan Rough is exactly that.

In the same category as Peter Shilton and Ray Clemence South of the border, he shows that although he may have lost some of his agility, he has gained in experience.

His professionalism and dedication sets a fine example to the club's young players.

Alan spent 13 memorable

ROUGH RIDES HIGH

years with Partick Thistle, gaining a First Division Championship medal and a League Cup winner's medal.

The Hampden triumph was something special. For Partick were given no chance against formidable Celtic, the clear favourites on the day, and sensationally ran out 4–1 winners.

Alan has often had to contend with unkind references to his surname, particularly before a game for Scotland against the old enemy, England, at Wembley in 1977.

No one was more pleased than Alan when he kept a clean sheet and Scotland scored two goals.

Having collected over a half-century of caps for his country, Alan is now concentrating on serving Hibernian for a good few years yet.

QUIZ

Think you're something of a football mastermind with a grasp of all aspects of the great game, from hard fact to off-beat trivia? Then take our test — and try to pass it with no 'passes' . . .
Answers on page 125

1: Has the entire Scotland World Cup Squad ever been voted 'Players of the Year' by the Scottish football writers?

2: Liverpool play at Anfield. Who play at Annfield?

3: Which new signing by Everton scored his first goal for the club — and incidentally his first-ever HEADED goal — to give the Goodison Park club a 1–0 win over Bradford City in last season's F.A. Cup Fourth Round?

4: His nickname is ''Pedro'' and he loves Mars bars. Name this striker.

5: Which famous manager was once capped at every level for England?

6: Know the four Football League clubs with plastic pitches?

7: In 1977–78 he kept goal in Nottingham Forest's victorious League Cup win, yet never played a League game for them. He's C--- W----?

8: Which country is the only one to have staged two World Cup Finals?

9: The European Football Championship is to be held in 1988. What was the original name of this tournament?

10: If you were the referee and a player, taking a throw-in, threw the ball directly into the opponents' goal, what award should you give?

11: How many substitutes are allowed in F.A. Cup matches?

12: Which Aston Villa player once played alongside Pele?

13: Which Zimbabwe international stars in the First Division?

14: Joe Payne holds the League record for scoring most goals in a game. It was for Luton v Bristol Rovers in 1936. Did he collect eight, nine or ten goals?

15: Arsenal left-back Kenny Sansom (left) came to Highbury in a straight exchange deal, valued at £1 million, from Crystal Palace. Who formed the other half of the deal?

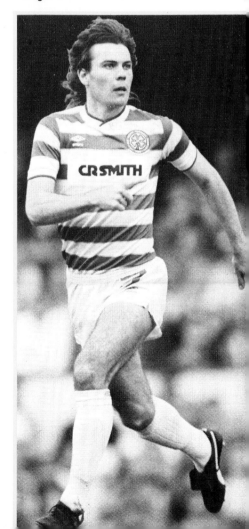

16: England once beat the fabulous Brazilians 2–0 in Rio de Janeiro (below). It happened in 1984. Who were the headline-hitting scorers?

17: December 13th, 1986, was a lucky day for Celtic striker Brian McClair (far right). He won his first cap for Scotland in a 3–0 win over Bulgaria, Luxembourg or Eire?

18: Gary Lineker, who hit a hat-trick against Poland, finished top scorer in the 1986 World Cup Finals. Was his total 6, 7 or 8 goals?

19: Is there a club in the Football League with a name beginning with 'K'?

20: England cricket captain Mike Gatting has a brother who played for Arsenal. Name him and the club he moved to from Highbury.

21: Sunderland and Southampton are F.A. Cup winning teams of 1972–3 and 1975–76. Sunderland beat Leeds United and Southampton toppled Manchester United (above). What is especially remarkable about their victories?

22: Can you name the very first signing made by Graeme Souness on taking over the player-manager role at Glasgow Rangers. (No, it wasn't Chris Woods or Terry Butcher!)

23: For what reason were Luton Town prevented from playing in last season's Littlewoods Cup Second Round?

24: TV personality Jimmy Greaves was one of the greatest-ever goalscorers to grace an English ground. He learnt his 'trade' at Chelsea, where he collected an impressive total of 132, 135 or 141 goals before moving to Spurs?

25: Which club are the longest-serving members of the Football League's First Division?

26: True or false? Manchester United once played at Maine Road, home of rivals Manchester City?

27: Who scored the goal that kept QPR in the Second Division in 1983? Clue: he's a winger and he once played for Chelsea.

28: Which clubs, apart from Arsenal, Spurs and Liverpool, have won the coveted double of F.A. Cup and League Championship?

29: Which was the first season in which three points were awarded for a win in the Football League?

30: Who was Scotland's most capped player before Kenny Dalglish?

31: Last season, Everton were the last First Division team to be beaten following the big kick-off, with a run of seven unbeaten games. Who turned them over 2–0?

32: Know the Watford player with the distinction of having scored in every Division?

33: Fourth Division Burnley were knocked out of last season's F.A. Cup in the First Round by which non-League side?

34: Another milestone from last season's First Division programme. At one spell early on in the season Norwich City went top of the First Division for the first time since 1979, 1982 or 1983?

35: Who said last season: ''When we lose we are negative and long ball. When we win, we are a lot of thugs.''?

FLASHBACK! FOREST

LIVERPOOL pipped by Forest for the League Championship and League Cup . . . respectability for Midlanders West Brom, Aston Villa, Coventry and Birmingham.

The famous Wolves managed to steer clear of relegation. But West Ham, Newcastle and Leicester plunged into the Second.

Bolton, now battling to get out of the Third Division won promotion to the First with Southampton and Spurs.

Rangers shocked their Old Firm rivals in Scotland and achieved a tremendous hat-trick of Championship, Scottish Cup and League Cup triumphs.

Now take a fascinating look back ten years ago and see how your favourites fared in League and Cup . . .

Footballer of the Year Kenny Burns in League Cup Final action at Wembley.

FIRST DIVISION FINAL POSITIONS 1977–78

	P	Home W	D	L	F	A	Away W	D	L	F	A	Total F	A	Pts
1. Nottingham Forest	42	15	6	0	37	8	10	8	3	32	16	69	24	64
2. Liverpool	42	15	4	2	37	11	9	5	7	28	23	65	34	57
3. Everton	42	14	4	3	47	22	8	8	5	29	23	76	45	55
4. Manchester City	42	14	6	1	46	21	6	8	7	28	30	74	51	52
5. Arsenal	42	13	5	3	38	18	8	5	8	22	19	60	37	52
6. West Bromwich Albion	42	13	5	3	35	18	5	9	7	27	35	62	53	50
7. Coventry City	42	11	4	6	33	18	7	6	8	42	44	75	62	46
8. Aston Villa	42	12	4	5	39	21	6	6	9	18	21	57	42	46
9. Leeds United	42	9	6	6	32	23	9	4	8	31	30	63	53	46
10. Manchester United	42	9	6	6	32	30	7	4	10	35	33	67	63	42
11. Birmingham City	42	10	7	4	37	24	3	4	14	18	36	55	60	37
12. Derby County	42	10	8	3	28	20	4	1	16	26	39	54	59	37
13. Norwich City	42	8	8	5	25	19	3	6	12	27	47	52	66	36
14. Middlesbrough	42	7	8	6	30	27	5	3	13	12	27	42	54	35
15. Wolverhampton Wanderers	42	7	11	3	28	28	5	1	15	23	36	51	64	36
16. Chelsea	42	7	11	3	28	20	4	3	14	18	49	46	69	36
17. Bristol City	42	6	9	6	32	24	5	4	12	17	29	49	53	35
18. Ipswich Town	42	8	5	8	27	26	3	8	10	20	35	47	61	35
19. Queens Park Rangers	42	6	7	8	31	28	4	8	9	16	36	47	64	33
20. West Ham United	42	8	6	7	31	28	4	2	15	21	41	52	69	32
21. Newcastle United	42	4	6	11	26	37	2	4	15	16	41	42	78	22
22. Leicester City	42	4	7	10	16	32	1	5	15	10	38	26	70	22

SECOND DIVISION FINAL POSITIONS 1977–78

	P	Home W	D	L	F	A	Away W	D	L	F	A	Total F	A	Pts
1. Bolton Wanderers	42	16	4	1	39	14	8	6	7	24	19	63	33	58
2. Southampton	42	15	4	2	44	16	7	9	5	26	23	70	39	57
3. Tottenham Hotspur	42	13	7	1	50	19	7	9	5	33	30	83	49	56
4. Brighton & Hove Albion	42	15	5	1	43	21	7	7	7	20	17	63	38	56
5. Blackburn Rovers	42	12	4	5	33	16	4	8	9	23	44	56	60	44
6. Sunderland	42	12	4	5	36	17	3	10	8	31	35	67	59	44
7. Stoke City	42	13	5	3	38	20	3	5	13	15	33	53	49	42
8. Oldham Athletic	42	9	7	5	31	20	4	9	8	23	24	54	58	42
9. Crystal Palace	42	9	10	2	32	19	4	5	12	19	27	51	46	41
10. Fulham	42	11	8	2	32	20	3	6	12	17	30	49	49	41
11. Burnley	42	13	4	4	38	22	2	5	14	18	42	56	64	40
12. Sheffield United	42	13	4	4	35	20	3	6	12	27	43	62	73	40
13. Luton Town	42	8	11	2	36	22	2	7	12	18	37	54	59	38
14. Orient	42	5	13	3	22	16	5	5	11	21	26	43	49	38
15. Notts County	42	6	9	6	36	27	5	2	14	18	41	54	68	38
16. Millwall	42	8	7	6	27	24	4	7	10	22	25	49	57	38
17. Charlton Athletic	42	10	4	7	38	27	3	8	10	17	41	55	68	38
18. Bristol Rovers	42	10	4	7	32	22	3	8	10	29	42	61	77	38
19. Cardiff City	42	12	6	3	35	25	1	6	14	18	46	53	71	38
20. Blackpool	42	7	8	6	30	24	1	12	8	29	49	59	60	37
21. Mansfield Town	42	6	9	6	23	25	1	8	12	18	44	49	69	31
22. Hull City	42	5	8	8	19	23	3	4	14	15	29	34	52	28

THIRD DIVISION FINAL POSITIONS 1977–78

	P	Home W	D	L	F	A	Away W	D	L	F	A	Total F	A	Pts
1. Wrexham	46	14	8	1	48	19	9	7	7	30	26	78	45	61
2. Cambridge United	46	19	3	1	49	19	4	9	10	23	40	72	51	58
3. Preston North End	46	16	5	2	48	19	4	11	8	15	19	63	38	56
4. Peterborough United	46	15	7	1	32	11	5	9	9	15	22	47	33	56
5. Chester	46	14	8	1	35	17	2	14	7	18	26	59	56	54
6. Walsall	46	12	8	3	35	17	6	9	8	26	33	61	50	53
7. Gillingham	46	10	11	2	36	14	5	9	9	31	38	67	60	50
8. Colchester United	46	14	6	3	40	21	5	9	9	27	38	64	57	48
9. Chesterfield	46	11	7	5	42	23	6	6	11	16	36	58	49	47
10. Swindon Town	46	11	11	1	39	19	5	4	14	28	38	67	57	47
11. Shrewsbury Town	46	13	6	4	32	26	4	7	12	31	34	63	57	47
12. Tranmere Rovers	46	10	9	4	32	26	6	5	12	22	38	59	52	46
13. Carlisle United	46	13	7	3	34	22	1	10	12	25	33	53	61	45
14. Sheffield Wednesday	46	11	7	5	34	25	4	8	11	16	26	50	52	45
15. Bury	46	10	8	5	32	18	3	10	10	30	41	49	59	44
16. Lincoln City	46	11	9	3	42	21	4	2	17	19	42	61	68	41
17. Exeter City	46	11	10	2	38	21	4	1	18	18	40	56	61	41
18. Oxford United	46	7	8	8	30	26	6	5	12	34	51	64	77	39
19. Plymouth Argyle	46	7	10	6	39	31	4	4	15	22	37	61	68	36
20. Rotherham United	46	11	5	7	26	19	1	13	9	18	44	44	63	36
21. Port Vale	46	7	11	5	28	33	1	9	13	16	35	44	68	36
22. Bradford City	46	11	6	6	38	24	1	5	17	18	62	56	86	35
23. Hereford United	46	9	9	5	28	22	0	4	19	9	37	37	79	31
24. Portsmouth	46	5	8	10	38	38	2	9	12	6	14	44	76	31

FOURTH DIVISION FINAL POSITIONS 1977–78

	P	Home W	D	L	F	A	Away W	D	L	F	A	Total F	A	Pts
1. Watford	46	18	4	1	44	14	12	7	4	41	24	85	38	71
2. Southend United	46	15	5	3	46	18	10	5	8	20	21	66	39	60
3. Swansea City	46	16	5	2	54	17	7	5	11	33	30	87	47	56
4. Brentford	46	15	6	2	50	17	6	8	9	36	37	86	54	56
5. Aldershot	46	15	8	0	45	16	4	8	11	22	31	67	47	54
6. Grimsby Town	46	14	6	3	30	15	7	2	14	27	41	57	51	50
7. Barnsley	46	15	4	4	44	20	3	10	10	17	29	61	49	50
8. Reading	46	12	6	5	43	22	6	8	9	12	31	55	52	50
9. Torquay United	46	9	9	5	33	21	7	6	10	24	35	57	56	47
10. Northampton Town	46	11	8	4	37	26	6	3	14	26	42	63	68	45
11. Huddersfield Town	46	11	8	4	37	28	4	7	12	26	36	63	55	45
12. Doncaster Rovers	46	14	4	5	39	26	2	10	11	11	37	50	61	45
13. Wimbledon	46	12	6	5	43	22	2	10	11	23	27	66	49	44
14. Scunthorpe United	46	9	8	6	31	23	5	8	10	19	26	50	55	44
15. Crewe Alexandra	46	14	6	3	43	22	1	9	13	22	47	50	69	45
16. Newport County	46	14	5	4	45	21	2	6	15	19	57	65	73	43
17. Bournemouth	46	14	4	5	41	19	2	6	15	11	31	52	59	41
18. Stockport County	46	10	8	5	36	23	6	3	14	19	41	55	51	43
19. Darlington	46	10	6	7	28	23	4	3	16	24	51	52	84	37
20. Halifax Town	46	7	11	5	28	24	3	7	13	24	52	52	76	38
21. Hartlepool United	46	11	5	7	29	28	4	2	17	22	58	51	84	37
22. York City	46	8	8	7	29	28	4	3	16	21	57	50	85	35
23. Southport	46	4	13	6	28	23	2	6	15	24	46	52	69	31
24. Rochdale	46	6	9	8	29	28	2	9	12	14	28	43	85	24

DOUBLE

Brian Clough and Peter Taylor — real Champions!

Footballer of the Year —
Kenny Burns (Nottm. Forest)
PFA Player of the Year —
Peter Shilton (Nottm. Forest)
Young Player of the Year —
Tony Woodcock (Nottm. Forest)
Bells Manager of the Year —
Brian Clough (Nottm. Forest)

League Cup Final 1977–78
Nottingham Forest 0
Liverpool   0 aet
Replay
Nottingham Forest 1 (Robertson pen)
Liverpool   0

FA Cup Final 1977–78
Ipswich 1 (Osborne)
Arsenal 0

RANGERS HAT-TRICK

Scottish League Cup Final 1977–78
Rangers 2 (Cooper, Smith)
Celtic   1 (Edvaldsson) aet

Scottish FA Cup Final 1977–78
Rangers   2 (MacDonald, Johnstone)
Aberdeen 1 (Ritchie)

Rangers celebrate Scottish F.A. Cup glory.

SCOTTISH PREMIER DIVISION FINAL POSITIONS 1977–78

	P	Home					Away					Total		
		W	D	L	F	A	W	D	L	F	A	F	A	Pts
1. Rangers	36	12	4	2	35	18	12	3	3	41	21	76	39	55
2. Aberdeen	36	14	1	3	43	13	8	6	4	25	16	68	29	53
3. Dundee United	36	9	4	5	28	17	7	4	7	14	15	42	32	40
4. Hibernian	36	10	5	3	35	16	5	2	11	16	27	51	43	37
5. Celtic	36	8	3	7	28	24	7	4	9	17	28	45	52	33
6. Motherwell	36	10	2	6	25	23	3	5	11	27	41	52	64	33
7. Partick Thistle	36	7	5	6	29	25	4	3	11	23	38	52	63	30
8. St. Mirren	36	8	3	10	17	28	4	13	7	31	23	64	24	
9. Ayr United	36	5	3	10	16	33	4	13	7	31	23	64	19	
10. Clydebank	36	5	3	10	16	33								

Goal difference applies when teams are level on points

SCOTTISH FIRST DIVISION FINAL POSITIONS 1977–78

	P	Home					Away					Total		
		W	D	L	F	A	W	D	L	F	A	F	A	Pts
1. Morton	39	12	5	2	45	23	13	5	1	40	19	85	42	58
2. Heart of Midlothian	39	13	4	2	37	18	11	6	3	40	24	77	42	58
3. Dundee	39	14	2	3	52	20	11	5	4	39	24	91	44	57
4. Dumbarton	39	7	8	1	38	20	9	5	5	27	28	65	48	49
5. Stirling Albion	39	7	8	4	29	16	6	5	9	23	30	52	46	42
6. Kilmarnock	39	10	5	5	40	27	4	7	10	33	43	52	64	40
7. Hamilton Academical	39	7	2	10	19	21	8	4	8	33	43	52	64	36
8. St. Johnstone	39	7	7	6	26	30	5	4	10	19	34	50	64	35
9. Arbroath	39	8	5	7	31	30	4	13	28	46	55	71	35	
10. Airdrieonians	39	10	5		27	25	4	13	28	31	55	71	29	
11. Montrose	39	6	7	6	28	41	2	14	16	43	44	84	24	
12. Queen of the South	39	6	7	6	28	41	2	14	16	43	44	84	24	
13. Alloa Athletic	39	4	7	9	22	27	4	15	17	47	39	74	19	
14. East Fife	39	4	7		22	27	4	15	17	47	39	74	19	

Goal difference applies when teams are level on points

SCOTTISH SECOND DIVISION FINAL POSITIONS 1977–78

	P	Home					Away					Total		
		W	D	L	F	A	W	D	L	F	A	F	A	Pts
1. Clyde	39	14	3	2	48	13	7	8	5	23	19	71	32	53
2. Raith Rovers	39	10	7	2	36	15	8	7	3	27	19	63	34	53
3. Dunfermline Athletic	39	11	6	2	41	14	6	6	7	27	28	51	46	48
4. Berwick Rangers	39	11	5	3	41	22	6	5	8	20	33	61	55	48
5. Falkirk	39	7	8	5	26	26	6	5	10	21	31	61	55	42
6. Forfar Athletic	39	12	3	4	40	24	5	7	7	33	42	68	68	40
7. Queen's Park	39	8	5	6	36	26	6	4	9	27	42	75	78	34
8. Albion Rovers	39	8	4	7	28	31	6	4	9	27	42	75	78	34
9. East Stirlingshire	39	8	2	10	38	33	4	11	21	34	54	65	30	
10. Cowdenbeath	39	8	3		33	29	4	11	21	34	39	43	67	30
11. Stranraer	39	7	7	6	26	28	4	12	23	54	43	89	22	
12. Stenhousemuir	39	7	4		20	35	4	12	23	54	43	89	22	
13. Meadowbank Thistle	39	6	2	3	28	32	2	3	15	17	41	45	73	20
14. Brechin City	39	5	3	11	28	32	2	3	15	17	41	45	73	20

Goal difference applies when teams are level on points

SOCCER BU

George Best, Denis Law and Bobby Charlton — united again! Mike Channon and Kevin Keegan back together!

No, SHOOT hasn't been in contact with Old Father Time. These legends ARE still in form, but for TV companies not clubs — and with their words not their feet. For them, life after the final whistle has been very good.

Being a TV personality or reporter, a Jimmy Greaves or a Danny Blanchflower, are just two of the options open to the Football League cream when age or long-term injury strike. But they are two among the very few which do not necessarily involve leaving the limelight.

There's coaching, or, better still, management. Perhaps even the chairmanship of the club to whom you devoted your playing career.

Or you could follow the lead of former Manchester United and England winger Gordon Hill, and link your football expertise and business sense. Along with Peter Shilton, Hill, apart from playing part-time for Northwich Victoria, is involved with a company called Plaspitch that specialises in goals for five-a-side and garden football.

Hostile crowd

But for the majority of ex-players, a new means of earning a livelihood lies on away ground — and in front of a hostile crowd to boot.

Even one-time international starlets find the transformation process difficult. Kevin Beattie, capped nine times by England and one of the lynchpins of Bobby Robson's star-studded Ipswich side of the late 70's, had cause to send an SOS call to the PFA to help him meet the mortgage payments on his house.

Beattie, now 34 and a father of three, admitted to depending on a friend's generosity in order to eat.

To PFA secretary Gordon Taylor, the plight which Beattie found himself in was tragic — but common.

"I get calls every day from lads with a big mortgage who suddenly find themselves out of work because of injury or loss of form," says Taylor. "A great number of them seem to forget that they only have an effective career lifespan of eight to ten years."

Left: Gordon Taylor wants clubs to do more for their ex-players.
Below: Former Manchester City and England star Frannie Lee is now a millionaire.
Right: Duncan McKenzie is also a successful businessman.

That's why the PFA set up a Benevolent Fund in 1970. Aided by the FA, the purpose of the fund was to relieve hardship cases and to do as much as financially possible towards eliminating the need for those Beattie-type hard luck tales that adorn the Sunday papers when news is scarce.

And, last year, 61 grants (value £31,500) were made to First and Fourth Division veterans alike.

And then there are the PFA's educational grants. Aimed at players of all ages, but particularly at teenagers, these grants enable players to study for further academic qualifications or to master another skill that they can use profitably after leaving the game.

Significant in more ways than one is the fact that the number of players who have benefitted from such assistance leapt by more than 30% between 1984 and 1985 — from 353 to 461 — and that the value of those benefits more than doubled.

Naturally, the combined costs of establishing a club community programme in the North-west of England and of extending YTS apprenticeships from one to two years, reduced those figures last year, but at least the players

SINESS

BE GOOD WHEN THE WHISTLE BLOWS....

are looking after their own kind. The clubs, according to Gordon Taylor, are simply not doing enough.

"We'd like full-time counsellors at every club in the League — but that should be the clubs' responsibility," believes Taylor. "But a third of them aren't interested in anything but football."

One man who has overcome the odds and become a star in another league, is Francis Lee, the blond bomber who strafed opposing nets for Bolton, Manchester City, Derby County and England during the 60's and early 70's.

While shooting his way towards

League Championship, FA Cup, League Cup, European Cup-Winners' Cup medals and 27 England caps, our Frannie was safeguarding his future.

Two years ago, Lee sold off part of his paper convertor company, F. H. Lee, for £8.5m, and retained a major stake as managing director. Ironically, he had originally asked one Gordon Taylor to join him in "a business venture" while the pair were at Bolton together.

"I was in charge of 120 employees as managing director, driving 45,000 miles a year and still managing to perform well in the First Division for Derby. I could have played for another couple of

seasons, but something had to give because I was only getting Sundays off," recalls Lee.

"What most players don't understand is that it costs you a lot of money to occupy yourself seven days a week when you're only working two hours a day. I never had that problem because, from the day I joined Bolton at 15, I always worked at some part-time job, whether it was mowing golf courses, cleaning gravestones or driving lorries."

Another forward to make a smooth transition has been Duncan McKenzie, a brilliant ball-juggler whose boots took him to Nottingham Forest, Everton, Leeds, Chelsea, not to mention Belgium and the USA — but never, unaccountably to some of us, to full England honours.

Radio star

These days Duncan mixes commentaries for his local station, Radio City, with running a delicatessen, an exotic fruit and veg store and a couple of flower shops.

"People sometimes refer to me in the same breath as Stan Bowles, Charlie George, Alan Hudson, football's supposed 'gay cavaliers'. A lot of football's victims have been the 'gay cavalier' type, but I had a stable background," says McKenzie.

"I married quite young — and well — and I never had any desire to live the high life," adds father-of-two McKenzie. "The game set me up. Clubs paid £1m for me in the days of the automatic signing-on fee, and I was careful not to waste that money."

MY FAVOUR

STEVE HUNT
Aston Villa

Schoolboy memory: Being picked to represent the Aston district at Junior level as a 9-year-old. I then graduated to the Seniors. The best part was travelling away to Cup matches.

Past player: In all my travels, including the spell I had at New York Cosmos playing with the likes of Pele, I've never seen a more gifted, magical player than George Best. He had everything.

Present player: You've probably never heard of him. He's a Yugoslav international and played for Red Star Belgrade. His name is Bogachievich and he operates in my position. Last I heard he was playing in America. He'd be a sensation in Britain, but no club could afford him!

Match: Gaining my first cap for England, when I came on as substitute in a 1–1 draw with Scotland at Hampden in 1984.

Training: Five-a-sides naturally. Like most players I like a change and play out of position — preferably behind the 'keeper!

Holiday: Touring with my family in our caravan. I enjoy the freedom. I hate being organised, so a package tour is definitely out.

Actor: Steve McQueen. He was tremendous in the car chase in 'Bullit'.

Actress: Natalie Wood, a real stunner.

Pop star: Bruce Springsteen. Showing my age here.

(Dream) car: The top of the Range Rover models. Four-wheel drive, built like a tank, and can go anywhere in style.

Meal: Home cooking (my wife is watching as I write this!).

Pastime: Walking my dogs. I used to practise Karate, but now my only sport is football.

TONY GALE
West Ham

Schoolboy memory: Playing for three different London districts. Unfortunately, it doesn't outweigh the memory of getting into the last 22 for England Schoolboys consideration, but failing to make the final 17!

Past player: Two, Peter Osgood and Alan Hudson — both Chelsea greats in the early Seventies. I was a mad-keen Blues fan when they helped Chelsea win the F.A. Cup and then the European Cup-Winners' Cup.

Present player: Alan Hansen, the Liverpool captain. Unlike many defenders, he's superb on the ball, taking his time, never getting flustered. A really cool customer.

Match: A promotion-clincher when I was at Fulham. It was the end of the 1981–82 season and we needed a point against Lincoln at home to go up into Division Two. Ranking level with that one is West Ham's 2–1 win over Ipswich in the closing stage of the 1985–86 season that allowed us to finish third in the First Division — The Hammers' highest-ever placing.

Training: Five-a-sides. Especially in the gym, where it's played at lightning speed.

Holiday: My family are in an enjoyable rut. Every summer we go to our favourite place, Marbella, and take an apartment.

Actor: Daniel J. Travanti, who plays Captain Frank Furillo in 'Hill Street Blues'. He's so convincing I can't believe he's acting.

Actress: Veronica Hamil, 'Miss Davenport', Furillo's lawyer wife. His perfect partner.

Pop star: Whitney Houston. I'm really gone on soul music.

(Dream) car: Mercedes two-seater sports. I really fancy myself in one.

Meal: Italian food with plenty of pasta.

Pastime: Swimming and golf. I'm not a member of a golf club, but I've won a few 'society' trophies.

Born: 7.11.63 Jamaica. Height: 5.11
First club: Sudbury Court (non—League)

ACHIEVEMENTS: He scored 16 League and Cup goals for his club in 1983—84 and played in the F.A. Cup Final that season. He scored two goals in England's runaway 8—0 victory over Turkey in a 1986 World Cup qualifying match.

Born: 25.10.63 Nottingham. Height: 5.8
First club: Nottingham Forest

ACHIEVEMENTS: He made 123 League appearances for Forest, scoring 30 goals. Made his England debut as sub against Russia in March 1986 and gained late place on England 'plane for Mexico.

Born: 20.11.61 Liverpool. Height: 6.0
First club: Liverpool

ACHIEVEMENTS: Left Liverpool for £50,000 in November 1980. Later figured in a £750,000 deal. Won first full England cap against Brazil in May 1984.

England striker Gary Lineker gives
of football friends. You

Who's my

Born: 10.1.54 Liverpool. Height: 5.11
First club: Liverpool

ACHIEVEMENTS: Played in the 1972 F.A. Youth Cup winning side. Won F.A. Cup winning medal for Manchester United in 1985. Won one England cap v. Luxembourg at Wembley in 1977.

Born: 12.7.58 London. Height: 5.11
First club: Southampton.

ACHIEVEMENTS: Six England caps since winning his first against Australia. Mainstay of a London club's midfield in 1986—87.

Born: 1.11.63 Wrexham. Height: 5.8
First club: Manchester United.

ACHIEVEMENTS: Scored 37 goals in first 89 League games. He emerged as a world class striker in 1984—85 when he scored 25 goals. This well-known personality plays regularly for Wales.

Born: 20.6.56 Huyton. Height: 5.8
First club: Bolton.

ACHIEVEMENTS: Turn pro with Bolton in May 1974 and chalked up 225 league games before joining First Division club for £60,000 in December 1982. Former England Under-21 player, he starred in England's 1986 World Cup campaign. Nine caps.

Three of Gary's soccer friends are seen in this happy Manchester United 1985 F.A. Cup winning team.

...you clues to his star gallery
...ave to guess their identities.

Mate?

ANSWERS ON PAGE 125

**Born: 27.10.57 Hayes. Height: 6.0
First club: Tottenham.**

ACHIEVEMENTS: One of the great midfield artists. He has made more than 350 League appearances. Approaching the 50-cap mark for England.

**Born: 24.9.57 Portsmouth. Height: 6.0
First club: Portsmouth.**

ACHIEVEMENTS: A member of the Brighton side beaten by Manchester United in the 1983 F.A. Cup Final. He has played for three First Division clubs, joining his current club November, 1984. He is a centre-half and has won three England caps.

**Born: 9.2.57 Edinburgh. Height: 5.6
First club: Dundee.**

ACHIEVEMENTS: Once described as 'the best player to come out of Scotland since Kenny Dalglish.' Commanded £500,000 transfer fee when sold by Scottish club to First Division club. Starred in Scotland's midfield in the 1986 World Cup Finals which were held in Mexico.

TOMMY'S TOP TEN

Warning to bosses- get Caton face the sack!

Tommy Caton has served under TEN managers in just SEVEN years!

As soon as 24-year-old Caton completed a £160,000 transfer to Oxford United from Arsenal, he joked: ''Maurice Evans, the Oxford manager, had better watch out. Wherever I go, managers seem to get the chop!''

Tommy Caton played over 200 games for Manchester City and became known as one of the most promising youngsters in the game. His play as a central-defender attracted all the big club scouts. And eventually Arsenal moved in to lure him to London in a £500,000 deal.

But Caton's astonishment in seeing so many managers take charge of Manchester City was to continue even when he got to North London.

''Tony Book was the one who signed me at Manchester City and then Malcolm Allison took over. When he went, John Bond became manager followed by John Benson. Then it was Billy McNeill and he sold me to Arsenal.

''Then Terry Neill, who had bought me for Arsenal, left the club and Steve Burtenshaw took charge for a while. Then Don Howe got the job . . . or was it the other way round!

After that, George Graham came in as the new manager and I later signed for Maurice Evans at Oxford.''

When Tommy Caton was in his prime at Manchester City, he was being tipped for a brilliant international future. He did get into the full England squad and became Terry Butcher's regular understudy for a time.

But then events at Arsenal conspired against him — and the name of Tommy Caton was gradually forgotten.

''Looking back, I never really wanted to leave Manchester City. At the time, I was mis-quoted and it came out that I had been desperate to get away.

A change

''That wasn't the case; it was just that I had been there five years and felt maybe a change would do me good and might enhance my England prospects.''

By the time Caton came to leave Arsenal, it was purely to play regular first team football at another club, something which had been denied him at Arsenal because the side had done so well in his absence.

''I was out for ten months at one stage and then had a blood disorder in pre-season training when it was a straight contest between myself and Tony Adams for the first team place alongside David O'Leary.

''I missed out and couldn't get back in when the side started winning.''

But Caton was so desperate to play first team football again that he rejected the offer of a new contract.

''I could have taken the easy way out, picked up my money and just hung around on the fringes. But that wasn't for me.''

So now Caton is an Oxford man, determined to re-build the promising career which seemed to wander off course, for a variety of reasons, at Highbury.

Rangers won the Premier Division for the first time since 1977-78. The Ibrox men are back at the top of Scottish football.

BRITAIN'S

Manager Graeme Souness brought in Englishmen Terry Butcher, Chris Woods and Graham Roberts and Rangers prospered.

BEST

ABOVE: Everton regained the League Championship trophy from Merseyside rivals Liverpool. LEFT: Kevin Sheedy played a prominent part in Howard Kendall's side's success with some superb displays in midfield.

Arsenal skipper Kenny Sansom holds aloft the first Littlewoods Cup trophy after their 2-1 win over Liverpool.

Gunners

Charlie Nicholas equalises Liverpool's early goal. Viv Anderson crossed from the right and the Scot was on hand to tap home from close range.

Glory

LEFT: Charlie celebrates his first goal with Tony Adams as Arsenal mount their challenge for their first trophy under George Graham's management. ABOVE: Nicholas strikes again seven minutes from time to win the Cup for The Gunners. His right foot shot is deflected by Ronnie Whelan past the stranded Bruce Grobbelaar to give Arsenal victory and Charlie the glory.

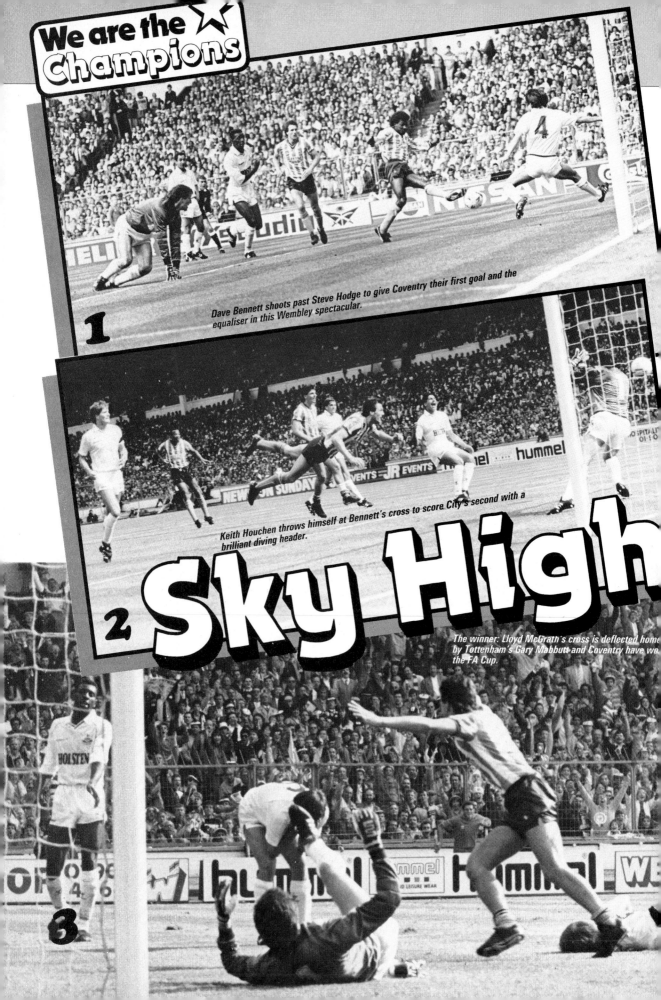

We are the Champions

Sky High

1 Dave Bennett shoots past Steve Hodge to give Coventry their first goal and the equaliser in this Wembley spectacular.

2 Keith Houchen throws himself at Bennett's cross to score City's second with a brilliant diving header.

The winner: Lloyd McGrath's cross is deflected home by Tottenham's Gary Mabbutt and Coventry have won the FA Cup.

3

Blues

We've won the Cup: Coventry revel in their Wembley triumph after winning their first
major trophy in 104 years.

We are the Champions

Ted McMinn, Ally McCoist and Terry Butcher celebrate Rangers winning the Skol Cup after their 2–1 win over Celtic.

SUPER

Ian Ferguson upset the form book with this left foot rocket as St. Mirren beat favourites Dundee United to win the Scottish Cup.

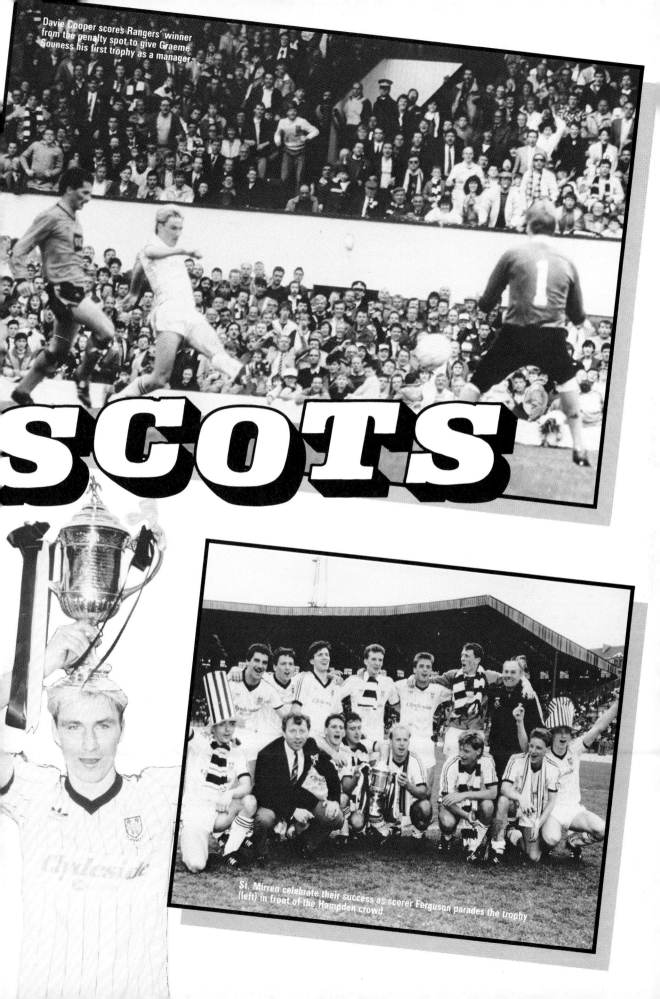

Davie Cooper scores Rangers' winner from the penalty spot to give Graeme Souness his first trophy as a manager.

SCOTS

St. Mirren celebrate their success as scorer Ferguson parades the trophy (left) in front of the Hampden crowd.

Ted Drake once scored seven goals for Arsenal in a match against Aston Villa but Luton's legendary Joe Payne hammered ten in a League game against Bristol Rovers on 13th April, 1936.

Ted MacDougall, who played for eight League clubs including Manchester United, West Ham and Norwich, scored nine goals for Bournemouth against Margate in an F.A. Cup-tie First Round match on 20th November, 1971.

Tottenham Hotspur pulled off the biggest First Division win since the War when they hammered ten goals into Everton's net on 11th October, 1958. By the way, Everton scored four in that match!

I don't believe it!

Ted Drake, Arsenal's deadly goalgetter, went on to manage Chelsea.

Arthur Rowley is the Football League's heaviest scorer of all time. He smashed 434 goals between 1946–65 (4 for WBA, 27 Fulham, 251 Leicester, 152 Shrewsbury). But Scottish striker Jimmy McGrory left Arthur's record for dead. Jimmy cracked 550 goals in an incredible career for Scotland, Celtic and Clydebank between 1922–38.

Wembley gets a regular 100,000 turn-out for the F.A. Cup Final. Twice that many watched the 1950 World Cup Final in Rio de Janeiro between Brazil and Uruguay. Official figure was 203,500.

Liverpool, managed by Joe Fagan, are the only British club to win three major trophies in one season. They picked-up the League Championship, European Cup and Milk Cup in 1983–84.

Everton were the first club to heat their pitch to beat the frost. They electrified Goodison Park in 1958.

A white ball was used for the first time in England in 1951.

Coventry fans watched their team win at Ninian Park, Cardiff . . . and they didn't travel a mile out of the city. The first closed circuit television broadcast of a match was

Liverpool won three major trophies in 1983–84, including the European Cup.

made from Cardiff in October 1965. More than 10,000 Coventry fans watched the screen.

Goal nets were used for the first time in a game between the North and the South in 1891.

The ten yard rule for free-kicks was introduced in 1913. Before that rule change, defenders could stand six yards from the kicker.

Gary Lineker's final school report said: "Too interested in sport. He'll never make a living playing football."

Only 4,554 people turned up to watch Arsenal play Leeds United at Highbury on May 5, 1966. The fixture clashed with Liverpool's European Cup-Winners' Cup Final match against Borussia Dortmund, which was screened live on television.

Clive Allen became the youngest £1m player when he left QPR for Arsenal at the age of 19.

Viv Anderson (right) (then Nottingham Forest) was the first black player to represent England at full cap level. He made his debut in 1978.

Spurs did not pay £100,000 for Jimmy Greaves (AC Milan) in 1961. They parted with £1 short of that figure, a mere £99,999.

Kevin Moran, of Manchester United, was the first player to be sent off in an F.A. Cup Final when he received his marching orders against Everton in May 1985.

1967 — England Manager Alf Ramsey is knighted for steering England to victory in the World Cup the previous year. His captain, Bobby Moore, received the OBE.

Newcastle United became the first club to win the F.A. Cup in three successive seasons when they beat Arsenal in the 1952 Final.

Pat Jennings holds the world record for international appearances. He played for Northern Ireland for 23 seasons, winning 119 caps after making his debut against Wales in April 1964.

No Welsh player has won 100 caps for his country. Nearest to the magic milestone is Joey Jones with 72.

Queens Park Rangers and Watford have twice applied for re-election to the Football League. Hartlepool

The fastest F.A. Cup Final goal was scored by Jackie Milburn of Newcastle United. 'Wor Jackie' (above) struck in just 45 seconds against Manchester City in 1955.

Mark Hateley (below) began his career at Coventry City. His father, Tony, once played for the Highfield Road outfit.

John Barnes, born in Jamaica on November 7th, 1963, was recommended to Watford by a supporter who had seen him playing in a local park.

England physiotherapist Norman Medhurst accepted his father, Harry's, invitation to become his assistant trainer at Chelsea on a temporary basis 'until something turned up'. Twenty years later, he was still there.

have made no fewer than 14 applications.

Workington applied for re-election to the Football League in 1977. They were refused entry and Wimbledon took over.

CROSSWORD

CLUES ACROSS:

(1) Graeme —, Everton striker. (5)
(4) Neil —, Man. City midfielder. (5)
(10) John —, Arsenal keeper. (5)
(11) — Park. Bolton's ground. (7)
(12) In short, the Scottish 1st Div. club from Broomfield Park. (7)
(13) — Park; ground of Dundee. (4)
(15) The 3rd, 6th & 8th Letters of Crystal Palace and the 9th, 10th & last letters of Scunthorpe United. (6)
(17) Bryan —, Manchester United captain. (6)
(20) — Gregory, Sheffield Wednesday midfielder. (4)
(21) — Park; ground of Stockport County. (7)
(24) Danny —, Southampton striker. (7)
(25) Trunk of the human body. (5)
(26) John —, Q.P.R. striker (below). (5)
(27) What is needed to complete S-----LAND? (5)

CLUES DOWN:

(2) Somebody who walks from the initial letters of Ipswich, Hull, Reading, Exeter and Kilmarnock. (5)
(3) Put on tape or video, for example! (8)
(5) Franz —, Nottm. Forest winger. (4)
(6) Ian —, Leicester 'keeper (right). (7)
(7) David —, Arsenal defender. (6)
(8) — Stadium; ground of Cambridge United. (5)
(9) They are changed at half-time! (4)
(14) Ray —, Oxford midfielder. (8)
(16) Awarded for a foul in this area! (7)
(18) Stuart —, W.B.A. keeper. (6)
(19) — Shilton, England 'keeper. (5)
(20) Halifax —, 4th Div. club. (4)
(22) Northern Ireland League club. (5)
(23) ----E ROAD; ground of Manchester City. (4)

ANSWERS ON PAGE 125

Goddard boosts Beardsley

Paul soon developed a good understanding with Peter Beardsley (right).

Swashbuckling goalscorers are a Newcastle tradition – the Geordies love 'em – and Paul Goddard's aim, since joining the club last season for a record fee, is to establish himself amongst their legendary ranks.

If he can stay clear of injury – and he's had more than his fair share of physical problems – Paul can achieve his ambition while helping to re-establish The Magpies amongst the finest clubs in Britain.

Shortly after the likeable Londoner moved to the North-East he found himself pitted against his old West Ham team-mates and starred in a sensational, TV-screened, 4–0 win.

His arrival sparked the Newcastle players, notably England international Peter Beardsley, who commented enthusiastically: "He's a quality player, with good touch and vision. He makes life easier for me."

Paul has always had an air of authority and confidence about him. His nickname of "Sarge" originates from his days as a Boys' Brigade N.C.O.

Many Newcastle fans believe that with his ability he'd command a place in any of their great sides of the past.

"But don't expect 30 goals-a-season from me," says Paul. "I'm not a natural goal-poacher. I don't care who scores as long as Newcastle win."

Here's hoping he can take the present side to a position that will justify the support of fans who are truly second to none . . .

GROAN

Perhaps the most embarrassing moment for any footballer is to see his attempted back pass or clearance sail past his own goalkeeper.

But giving away own goals can prove extremely costly as well as embarrassing as Liverpool will testify.

Two own goals conceded in the 1986 Milk Cup Semi-Final, second leg at Anfield cost them a place in the Final.

'Goals' by Ronnie Whelan and Gary Gillespie gave QPR a 2—2 draw on the night, sending them to Wembley 3—2 on aggregate.

Gary Gillespie summed up the Anfield players' feelings after the match: ''We gave them the game.

''We got the two goals that we needed and then handed them two silly ones.''

Gary had inadvertently turned Wayne Fereday's low cross past goalkeeper Bruce Grobbelaar in an attempt to stop former team-mate Mike Robinson reaching the substitute's cross. That mistake in the dying minutes of the game set

Noel Blake's fatal back pass ended Pompey's unbeaten run.

Rangers up for their Wembley date against Oxford United.

''All I saw was Jim Beglin attempting to clear,'' says Whelan. ''The ball cannoned off me and into the net. That's all I know about it. I felt sick, we all did.''

If those two own goals had denied Liverpool a trip to the famed twin towers then spare a thought for poor Tommy Hutchison, now manager of Swansea City.

Playing for Manchester City against Tottenham in the 1981 FA Cup Final, Tommy had put his side ahead, scoring from a Ray Ranson cross.

City were well on their way to winning the 100th Cup Final when, nine minutes from time, disaster struck.

Spurs' Glenn Hoddle took a free-kick just outside the City penalty-area that looked as though it would not trouble goalkeeper Joe Corrigan.

The ball went over the City wall, but was travelling wide when Hutchison, who had taken up a position just behind the defensive line-up, tried to head the ball clear. He only succeeded in sending Corrigan the wrong way and the ball into the corner of the net.

Spurs held out in extra-time and went on to win the replay 3—2.

Hutchison had become only the second player in history to achieve that unenviable feat in an FA Cup Final. Bert Taylor of Charlton scored for both sides when Derby won 4—1 in 1946.

GOALS

Glenn Hoddle's shot is deflected by Tommy Hutchison during the 100th F.A. Cup Final.

In 1984—85 Wimbledon scored a goal without even touching the ball. Alan Cork had put them 1—0 up in a League match at home to Portsmouth just before half-time.

Pompey restarted and central-defender Noel Blake rolled the ball back to goalkeeper Alan Knight without looking. Knight, who had been injured trying to prevent Cork's opening goal, was attending to a knock on his knee and did not see the back pass either.

The result was that the ball trickled past him and into the unattended net. Wimbledon went on to win 3—2 and that result cost Portsmouth their unbeaten record.

Another victim was Manchester City's Nicky Reid. Playing against Chelsea at Stamford Bridge poor conditions made it very difficult for all concerned.

City goalkeeper Eric Nixon had kept Chelsea's dangerous strike force of Kerry Dixon and David Speedie at bay all afternoon . . . but he had not reckoned on his right-back Reid.

In the closing minutes, with the game heading for a goalless draw, Kevin McAllister threw a hopeful ball into the City area. Jerry Murphy headed on.

Unchallenged, Reid tried to guide the ball back to Nixon, who had come out for the throw.

Another example of football's power to turn champs into chumps.

COPPELL'S TARGET

But all that doesn't stop Coppell wishing he was a First Division regular again. He has been once before — as a top class player with Manchester United, with whom he forged a reputation as an outstanding wingman who went on to play for England.

He says: "I admit I do get spells where I miss the First Division. I'd much rather be fighting for my life up there than sitting among the leaders in the Second."

Coppell has had a tough task since taking over at Selhurst Park. It has been his first taste of management since quitting the game through injury. And he joined a club in a desperate financial position which requires careful housekeeping for years to come.

Problem

"If you owe more than £1m. and all you can put in against that is £20,000 or £30,000 here and there, it takes a long time to make up that million. That is the problem."

So Coppell has been able to buy precious few players and even those have been cut price bargains. The big money stars have been conspicuous by their absence from Selhurst Park and the Palace headquarters.

Coppell has always said: "If we had a clear bank balance, Palace would get promotion immediately. But I am in the

Palace to rule in the First!

Steve Coppell reckons there is only one place for an ambitious player or manager to be in football and that's the First Division.

Not even the nightmare example of Crystal Palace's Selhurst Park ground-sharing rivals Charlton Athletic in season 1986/87 deters Coppell from that view.

The young Palace manager says: "I'm well aware that Charlton struggled in their first season back in Division One. They found that there is a certain formula to get out of the Second Division but it doesn't necessarily bring you survival in the First."

So Charlton, promoted in May 1986, chased points like drowning men thrashing around for lifejackets, as their First Division season hit major problems in 1986–87. Big money signings had to be made — it was a season of immense problems for the club.

same position as 80 other managers in the Football League and so I am not complaining."

Steve Coppell considers Second Division football as different as if it were foreign football. "It is a hard Division to judge standards by because it is as if it's a totally different standard of football from the First."

Will Steve Coppell go on to become one of our leading managers in the English Football League?

It's hard to tell. But what is certainly NOT in doubt is that the articulate, shrewd Palace boss has had a thoroughly realistic grounding in the world of football management at Crystal Palace.

Marwood's a menace

T he sight of Sheffield Wednesday's little winger, Brian Marwood tormenting the defences of Luton and Watford with his quicksilver speed and tantalising skill is especially agonising for the fans of those two clubs.

For their managers turned down the chance to snap him up from Third Division Hull in the summer of 1984 for £125,000.

Instead, Wednesday boss Howard Wilkinson snapped up a bargain buy whose value on the transfer market has escalated to at least five times the original too.

Brian showed his true worth in front of millions of TV viewers glued to their sets last season for a thrilling clash between Wednesday and Champions Liverpool.

He earnt rave reviews, including one from TV football expert Mike Channon, who voted him man of the match.

Brian isn't just a goal-maker, he can score them, too, as his 13 League goals in season 1985–86, making him the club's top scorer, amply testifies.

His biggest disappointment? Being placed on standby for an England game against Egypt and not getting the call.

"I made the mistake of building up my hopes so much that disappointment caused my game to suffer for a month afterwards."

That setback will be just a dim memory if Brian realises his dream of ousting his England rivals for the wing position and flies high for his country in the coming European Championships.

Mark suits Watford and vice versa!

Mark Falco can't help laughing when he thinks how close he came to turning down his move to Watford last year.

The powerful striker knew he was no longer wanted at Tottenham, but was reluctant to accept the fact and stalled when Watford came in with a £350,000 bid for him.

He thought it over, swallowed his pride and accepted Graham Taylor's challenge. And now he's loving life at Vicarage Road.

Thanks to superb service from Worrell Sterling and David Bardsley, Falco's tremendous aerial power has never been put to better use.

At Spurs he managed 68 goals in 173 League appearances, a creditable enough performance from a man who never enjoyed the adulation given to most White Hart Lane stars.

Now he's averaging a goal every other game and, as Graham Taylor says: "Mark will probably never play for England, but he'll score a lot more First Division goals than some of the strikers who do."

QPR defender Alan McDonald can safely look forward to becoming one of the most capped Northern Ireland internationals in history.

The first of the 'new wave' of Ulstermen, McDonald's commanding presence and admirable will to win have made him a permanent choice in the famous green shirt.

And with another seven or eight years left in him, he can expect to collect well over 50 caps.

1 Peter Shilton was born in Leicester on September 18, 1949, the second of three sons to Les and May Shilton. His brothers are Tony and Graham.

2 The Shiltons lived above Les's grocery shop on a tough council estate in the Leicester suburb of Braunstone, but later moved to a quieter area to give Peter more peace before matches.

3 Shilton first played in goal at the age of nine and was soon recognised as a brilliant prospect, but as a young teenager Shilton feared he wouldn't grow sufficiently to become a goalkeeper. To combat this he would spend time each day lying on the floor while straining his arms and legs to touch chalk marks made above his hands and below his feet. He even swung from bannisters with weights tied to his feet.

4 Consequently Shilton's arms are now two inches longer than is normal for a man of his build. Most of his shirts and jackets are specially made.

5 From an early age Shilton took great pride in his training. He perfected, for

Peter's super save helped Nottingham Forest beat Hamburg in the 1980 European Cup Final.

The great Gordon Banks.

example, 12 different methods of punching a ball to suit every occasion.

6 He has also been obsessed with physical training to sustain a peak level of fitness throughout his career. He once worked with an Army PTI, leading to nicknames including 'Powerful Pierre' and 'Tarzan'.

7 Shilton was the youngest player ever to appear for Leicester in a competitive match when he made his League debut against Everton in May 1966 aged 16 years 228 days.

8 Shilton's brilliance soon led to Leicester selling their other 'keeper Gordon Banks — who at the time was regarded as the World's best — to Stoke City for £52,000 in April 1967.

9 Leicester's local newspaper, The Mercury, soon received numerous letters complaining about "this kid who was ordering defenders around as if he was the manager."

10 Shilton and his wife Sue were married in September 1970.

They now have to sons, Michael (14) and Sam (9). The family has a pet golden retriever named Jasper.

11 His attention to detail in his preparation for games is matched during his private hours. He's extremely houseproud, for example, and moans at Sue if the dog moults on the family carpet. "Can't we clear this up," he says. "I think if you are tidy in little things you'll be tidy in big things."

12 The Shiltons now live in a fantastic four bedroom detached home in Chilworth, Hampshire. They also have a cottage in the Devon village of Bigbury, near Plymouth.

13 Shilton has played for four League clubs, and his three transfers have cost the buying clubs a total of £950,000. When he left Leicester in November 1974 Stoke paid £325,000 for him, then a world record fee for a goalkeeper. Nottingham Forest then signed Shilton for £300,000 in September 1977, and he later became the first footballer in Britain to earn £100,000 a year at Forest. Southampton paid

ILTON

£325,000 for Shilton in August 1982.

14 Shilton has also appeared for England at Schoolboy, Youth, Under-23 and senior international levels and, on October 1985, beat Gordon Banks' record of 73 caps for an England 'keeper. He is now well on the way to the century.

15 It is Shilton's intention to carry on playing until he is 40, before moving into management. Shilton's ultimate ambition is to become the manager of England.

16 His favourite newspaper is the Sporting Life, reflecting his great love of racing. Shilton once bought some greyhounds and trained them himself, and later owned racehorses, including Admiral Jersey, Dark Hope, Twice A Star (he half shared this horse) and Prickles.

17 Shilton rates a goal by Jimmy Greaves, for Tottenham against Leicester in the 1960's, as the best goal ever scored against him. Greaves weaved past three Leicester defenders on a diagonal run from the right touchline and then rounded Shilton before tucking the ball in the net. ''The crowd was still applauding Greaves when we re-started the game,'' Shilton recalls.

18 He has more difficulty picking out his greatest save. But he is particularly proud of one stop from Hamburg's Bernd Nogly for Nottingham Forest in the 1980 European Cup Final. Nogly struck his shot from 30 yards, and the ball swerved right and then left, forcing Shilton to change direction and his saving hand in mid-air to push the ball away with his right hand.

19 Apart from saving goals, Shilton managed to get on the scoresheet himself with a high drop kick for Leicester against his present club Southampton during the 1967–68 season.

20 He did, in fact, once play centreforward for Leicester in a testimonial match against Derby, then managed by Brian Clough. Shilton didn't manage to score on that occasion. Clough later managed Shilton at Forest, and reveals: ''I bet that given the choice Shilton would have wanted to be a centre forward.''

Norman Whiteside, the youngest player to appear in the World Cup Finals, has another record in his sights. With nearly 200 League appearances under his belt and another ten years of his career to go, Whiteside could well overtake Bobby Charlton's proud achievement of 606 games for Manchester United.

Paul Simpson is one of the most frustrating players in the game. Who says so? Manchester City boss Jimmy Frizzell, who complains: ''Paul can beat any full-back going when he's on song, but he is so inconsistent.'' Many rival managers would love to have his problem!

RAY CLEMENCE

This Is Your Life!

The red book is presented, TV style, to the Tottenham and former England and Liverpool goalkeeper.

Ray Clemence, you were the safest pair of hands in the game behind that rock-like Liverpool defence that held so steady as The Reds stormed to so many triumphs in Europe during the 1970's.

Ray, may I quote Bob Paisley, your Liverpool manager at the time, who paid you this glowing tribute in his book.

Asked to choose his all-time Best Liverpool XI, he wrote this judgment: ''Possibly the goalkeeping position was the easiest for me to settle, because it really boiled down to two contenders, Tommy Lawrence and Ray Clemence.

''I don't feel I am doing Tommy any injustice in picking Ray as my No. 1 for the last line of defence. Ray's record of consistency with Liverpool and England, gives him the edge.''

Ray Clemence . . . this is your life! You were born on August 8th, 1948 in Skegness and began to make your mark as a Notts County amateur.

Your big break came in the season that led to England winning the World Cup when you made four appearances for Scunthorpe in the 1965–66 season.

You won a regular place in the Scunthorpe first team the following season and went on to play 48 games before the great Bill

Shankly took you to Liverpool for £15,000.

Ray Clemence . . . this is your life! You did not rise to instant stardom at Anfield. Indeed, for two full seasons you understudied Tommy Lawrence before making your first-team debut in 1969–70 and winning a regular first team place the following season.

Now, your career began to take-

off. Never a flashy goalkeeper, always relying on sound positional play, a courage that no coach can teach.

You performed superbly in four England Under-23 outings before winning your first full England cap against Wales in November 1972.

Champions of Europe. Ray proudly holds the European Cup aloft after helping defeat Bruges 1–0 at Wembley in May 1978. It was Liverpool's second consecutive triumph in the competition.

Ray, your team-mates that day in Cardiff were Peter Storey, Emlyn Hughes, Norman Hunter, Roy McFarland, Bobby Moore, Kevin Keegan, Martin Chivers, Rodney Marsh, Colin Bell and Alan Ball.

What's more, you won the game 1–0 . . . Colin Bell the scorer.

You played in the next game, against Wales again on your Wembley debut, but Peter Shilton was to win 15 caps before you next had a game, against East Germany in Leipzig.

Now, it was your turn, Ray, to keep Shilton in the shade . . . and it was not long before you had overtaken him in the cap-winning stakes as Liverpool took Europe and the domestic competitions by storm.

You were one of the five Liverpool players who took part in the first three European Cup Finals and in 1978–79 you gave historians of the great game a jewel.

Ray, you clearly won't forget that in playing all 42 League games for Liverpool you let in only 16 goals, arguably the best defensive record in football.

You won five Championships with Liverpool, two League Cup wins, one F.A. Cup and three European Cup winners medals and two UEFA Cup successes.

You left your beloved Anfield in August 1981 when Tottenham Hotspur laid out a cool £300,000.

Along came another Cup winning medal and a League Cup runners-up medal and you recorded your 700th Football League appearance in the 1985–86 season.

But your record at home is only marginally greater than your reputation abroad after winning 61 glorious caps in a brilliant England career.

Ray Clemence, great goalkeeper and one of the great sportsmen of our times, THIS IS YOUR LIFE!

Great save as Ray gathers the ball from QPR striker Simon Strainrod in the 1982 F.A. Cup Final replay which Spurs won 1–0.

A classic save against Brazil at Wembley in 1981. Bad news . . . Ray was captain. Good news . . . England lost 1–0.

Inchy's miles ahead

Graeme Sharp (left) formed a deadly partnership with Gary Lineker and kept Adrian out of the Everton side.

Graeme scored more than 60 goals between them in one season. There was no way he could drop one of them to make room for me.

"Reluctantly, I came to the decision that I had reached the end of the road at Everton and asked to be placed on the transfer list.

"But Gary's move to Spain changed all that."

Now Heath is once again turning in the kind of performances which took him to the brink of the England squad before his devastating knee injury.

Ironically, he could even become Lineker's international partner in Bobby Robson's team.

But it's not just on the pitch that Heath is looking to improve his image.

He says: "Players have got to realise the influence we can have on people who go to football matches.

"We have to show more responsibilty both on and off the pitch. We must make better use of the media to put our views across. Many pages are devoted to sport each day and we can have a positive influence on the people who read them."

Up-market

He's also altering the traditional footballer's image by putting his money into an up-market wine bar in his home town of Newcastle-under-Lyme in Staffordshire.

"I moved to Liverpool shortly after my transfer from Stoke, but my house was burgled twice, my car was stolen a couple of times and I just couldn't settle in the area.

"A lot of footballers open a pub when they retire from the game, but I decided I wanted to try something a bit different.

"With the help of my dad, I completely renovated an old shop and turned it into a Continental style wine and cocktail bar called 'Heroes'?.

"It's been a tremendous success so far and I'm even thinking of opening another bar. But I don't want to get too involved in it just yet.

"I'm concentrating on my game, on scoring goals for Everton and improving my partnership with Graeme Sharp."

The Sharp-Heath combination is already one of the deadliest double-acts in British soccer.

It's not surprising that the man they call 'Inchy' has a giant following in football.

It was a sad day for British football when England ace Gary Lineker turned his back on the Football League for the sun and pesetas of Barcelona.

But Adrian Heath admits he was glad to see the back of the man who was top scorer in the 1986 World Cup Finals.

Explains Heath: "Gary's £2.8 million transfer to Barcelona saved my Everton career.

"I never wanted to leave Goodison Park, but I would have done just that if Gary had not left before me."

Heath is quick to point out that there was nothing personal between him and goal ace Lineker.

"We got along famously. Gary is a smashing lad. But while he was in the Everton team, there was no place for me."

The problem all stemmed from the fact that Heath had been sidelined for the best part of a year by a serious knee injury which at one stage had threatened his career.

During his absence, Everton boss Howard Kendall paid £800,000 for Lineker, who struck up such a devastating partnership with Graeme Sharp there was no room for Heath when he finally recaptured full fitness.

"I couldn't blame the boss," admits Adrian. "Gary and

Graham Roberts couldn't have wished for a more spectacular debut performance for Rangers.

A few days after his £450,000 transfer from Tottenham, Roberts earned an immediate nickname from a sell-out Ibrox attendance when he set off on a sensational solo run against Dundee United.

Players seemed to melt in front of him as he swept past four defenders in a death-or-glory raid on Billy Thomson's goal.

With a posse of players trailing behind him, Roberts burst into the box, hit a drive against the outcoming Thomson and Ally McCoist followed up to slide the ball in for the first goal in a 2—0 triumph.

The Ibrox faithful roared their approval

Graham
JAW

of their latest English import and immediately labelled him 'Jaws II'.

Sturdy Tom Forsyth, straight from the same no-nonsense, no-surrender mould, won undying fame as 'Jaws I' from the Rangers supporters in the Seventies. Roberts has moved smoothly into his boots as the Ibrox Iron Man.

"I've always played my football to win," says Roberts. "Even when I was non-League with Weymouth I always gave it my best shot.

"I'm not interested in being second-best to anyone. That's why I jumped at the chance of joining Rangers.

"Graeme Souness's will to win has never been in doubt and he has impressed everyone at the way he has tackled this job."

The fanatical support of the Rangers following is still something that takes Roberts's breath away.

"They're unbelievable," he says. "The atmosphere they can create is fantastic. They are magnificent fans.

"Of course, they are demanding. Why not? They deserve the best and it's our intention to give them what they want. They pay our wages after all."

Roberts, 29, is believed to be on £2,000-per-week plus perks and bonuses at Ibrox and he stresses: "This is no step back for me. The

Premier Division is every bit as competitive as the English First Division.

"The top five or six clubs could certainly do well across the border. And when the Premier Division is trimmed back to ten teams again at the end of the season it will make it even more competitive. Great!"

It hasn't been sunshine all the way in Scotland for hard man Roberts. For instance, don't mention Hamilton Accies. 'Jaws II' might growl at the sound of their name. And no wonder!

Playing in only his fifth game for Rangers last season, he was booked and then sensationally ordered off against the Douglas Park part-timers in a League match at Ibrox.

Two weeks later Hamilton were back at Ibrox, this time on Scottish Cup duty, Roberts was back after an automatic one-game suspension and although he was probably Rangers' outstanding performer that wintry afternoon, he couldn't prevent them from losing 1–0.

Roberts-
S II

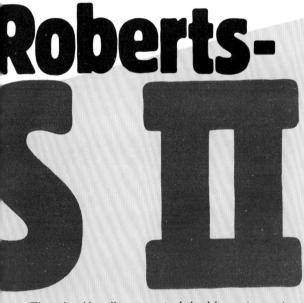

That day Hamilton created the biggest upset in the history of the Scottish Cup.

Roberts was at Hampden last season as a spectator, with his — then Spurs colleagues Richard Gough and Chris Waddle, to see Rangers beat Celtic 2–1 and lift the League Cup. He had hoped to be involved last May during the Scottish Cup Final at the same venue.

"It wasn't to be," sighs the rugged utility player. "But there's always this season!"

Graeme Souness is determined to give Rangers fans plenty to cheer about.

DIEGO MARADONA

Diego Maradona is simply the best player in the world producing some outstanding displays in the 1986 World Cup Finals.

1. Did Diego start his career at Boca Juniors, Argentinos Juniors or River Plate?

2. After a spell in Barcelona, Maradona signed up for which Italian side?

3. The Argentinian scored some great goals in helping his country win the 1986 World Cup but what was so controversial about his first goal against England?

4. He scored both goals in a Semi-Final of the '86 tournament. Who were the victims?

5. In 1982, in Spain, Maradona was sent-off against which South American side?

JESPER OLSEN

Denmark's Jesper Olsen is one of the most frustrating players in the game. On his day he can leave defenders dead with his trickery, but he lacks consistency.

1. Which famous Dutch club did Olsen leave to join Manchester United in 1984?

2. How many goals did Jesper score for Denmark in the 1986 World Cup Finals?

3. Two of Olsen's Danish team-mates are currently playing for teams in the First Division. Name the players and their clubs.

4. Olsen scored a superb goal against England in a European Championship match in Copenhagen. In what year was the match played?

5. Which manager signed Olsen for United?